rest

rest

Living in Sabbath Simplicity

keri wyatt kent

ZONDERVAN®

ZONDERVAN.com/
AUTHORTRACKER
follow your favorite authors

ZONDERVAN®

Rest
Copyright © 2009 by Keri Wyatt Kent

Requests for information should be addressed to:
Zondervan, *Grand Rapids, Michigan* 49530

Library of Congress Cataloging-in-Publication Data

Kent, Keri Wyatt, 1963–
    Rest : living in Sabbath simplicity / Keri Wyatt Kent.
      p. cm.
    Includes bibliographical references.
    ISBN 978-0-310-28597-7 (softcover)
    1. Rest—Religious aspects—Christianity. 2. Sabbath. 3. Simplicity—Religious
aspects—Christianity. I. Title.
BV4670.K46 2009
263'.1—dc22
                                     2008042830

All Scripture quotations, unless otherwise indicated, are taken from the *Holy Bible, Today's New International Version™. TNIV®.* Copyright © 2001, 2005 by International Bible Society. Used by permission of Zondervan. All rights reserved.

Scripture quotations marked MSG are taken from *The Message.* Copyright © 1993, 1994, 1995, 1996, 2000, 2001, 2002. Used by permission of NavPress Publishing Group.

Internet addresses (websites, blogs, etc.) and telephone numbers printed in this book are offered as a resource to you. These are not intended in any way to be or imply an endorsement on the part of Zondervan, nor do we vouch for the content of these sites and numbers for the life of this book.

Interior design by Beth Shagene

Printed in the United States of America

08 09 10 11 12 13 • 23 22 21 20 19 18 17 16 15 14 13 12 11 10 9 8 7 6 5 4 3 2 1

For my readers,
whose questions inspired me to write this book
and whose stories fill its pages

contents

introduction

Living in Sabbath Simplicity

Are you tired? Worn out? Burned out on religion?
Come to me. Get away with me and you'll recover your life.
I'll show you how to take a real rest.
—Jesus (Matt. 11:28 MSG)

Sunday morning. I am groggy, staring out the window over the sink, listening to the gurgle of the coffeemaker and the chirping of the birds outside my drafty window. My children watch *Arthur* on public television, eating Pop-Tarts on the couch. My husband, at the pine table in the kitchen, eats from a cereal bowl resting on the open pages of the *Chicago Tribune* sports section as he reads it—his daily ritual, as critical to his well-being as the coffee is to mine. I pour cream, then coffee—just the smell of it begins to clear the cobwebs in my brain—and gently remind all three of them to get dressed for church soon.

"Mom?" my nine-year-old asks.

"Yes, Aaron," I say, sipping coffee, leaning against the kitchen counter.

"What do we *have* today?" He'd heard some of his friends saying things like, "I can't play, I have soccer," or "I have piano lessons today." So his question is really, What's on the agenda today? What do we *have* to do?

"Well, buddy, today is Sunday," I say. "What do you think we have?"

He chews his Pop-Tart thoughtfully, then calmly replies, "Peace."

I look at him over the rim of my mug. I set the mug on the counter, raise my arms in silent victory: after several years of trying to make our Sundays a Sabbath, a true day of rest, my kids are getting it. They say values aren't just taught but caught, and my little boy has just shown me the ball in his mitt.

"You're right, buddy," I say, smiling at him. "That's exactly what we have."

real life intrudes

That Sunday, we did have peace. After church, the kids and I (and a friend or two of theirs) had some soup, played board games, hung out. The day was marked more by what we left undone than what we did. On purpose, we did not go shopping, do laundry, do housework, or turn on the computer. I didn't cook an elaborate meal; we ate leftovers for dinner. When the kids wanted my attention, I gave it. When they didn't, I read the Sunday paper or a book. We simply relaxed. Well, the kids and I did. My husband, who works as a realtor, showed houses for part of the day.

But during soccer season, which we're in the midst of right now, the picture looks a little different. Actually, it feels like we're a different family. This time of year, I'm a stressed-out soccer mom seeking Sabbath. Yesterday, for example, was Sunday. My daughter played in a local soccer tournament. Her game began at 10:30 a.m., which meant she had to be on the field by 10:00 a.m., making it impossible to attend either the 9:00 a.m. or 11:00 a.m. service at church. Parents were required to work shifts at the tournament to help run it, so my husband took an early morning shift, and I took an afternoon shift. Our family moved in all different directions. We didn't rest, really. We didn't connect or even pause. It felt like any other busy day.

So do we practice Sabbath or not? If we have Sundays that sometimes fall apart or don't seem very restful, why even try?

Well, suppose I were telling you about another spiritual practice—say, for example, Bible study—and I told you that studying Scripture had changed my life, that I had encountered God in the practice of reading his Word. But suppose I admitted that there are times I don't understand parts of what I read. That I have not yet fully grasped everything there is to know about the Bible. That I sometimes doubt its veracity, wonder about its relevance. Would you advise me to give up this practice because I have yet to do it perfectly?

Like study or solitude or prayer, Sabbath-keeping is a spiritual practice. Some weeks are better than others, but we continue to practice it because in it, we encounter God in life-changing ways. When we see Sabbath-keeping as a spiritual practice, we realize that we don't need to "institute" it. We simply need to practice it and invite others to join us. We can be intentional without becoming institutional.

But Sabbath-keeping is more than just a practice to draw us closer to God. It is also a command, and not just a minor ceremonial law but one of the Ten Commandments. Now, a number of public-opinion polls in recent years have pointed out that although the majority of Americans say they believe in the Ten

Commandments, most can't name five of them. So if we say we are trying to live biblically, to live according to God's will, what should our Sundays (or perhaps our Saturdays) look like?

I personally have tried to practice Sabbath since the children were small, with varying degrees of success. Much of the time, although definitely not all of the time, it is a day, as my son says, of peace. Of restfulness, of recreation that actually re-creates us. A day which almost always includes some activity, yet remains a respite from hurry and chaos. A day when we focus on one another instead of on our to-do lists. Still, we never have perfect Sundays. Thank God. Because often, what I need to rest from most is my perfectionism.

As I've shared my Sabbath journey in magazine articles and blogs, I have often received uninvited critiques of what I do or don't do. I've been told, among other things, that I should not take my kids to Dairy Queen on Sundays (because it forces the employees there to work on the Sabbath), that I should not let my daughter play soccer on Sundays, and that I practice on the wrong day. I consider these prayerfully. Here's the thing, though. The Bible says nothing about soccer, but it does say you shouldn't light a fire on Sabbath (Exod. 35:3). How many of the people who point fingers at my recreational activity violate the strict biblical rules about Sabbath by using electricity or driving a car (all, according to Orthodox Judaism's strict interpretation of the Bible, prohibited by this passage)?

My goal in Sabbath-keeping is not legalism or empty ritual or even making Sabbath a perfect day. (Good thing, since I'm obviously pretty far from accomplishing that.) In it, I see an opportunity to focus my energy on what Jesus says are the two most important commandments: to love God and to love others. Although our culture often advises us to take time for ourselves, that's not the heart of Sabbath. While time for yourself is nice, the most meaningful Sabbath practices are focused on God and others. To take a day to put aside our cares and our work so we can just love God and love others—that's the heart of resting in God, the key to recovering our lives.

As I have wrestled with how to practice Sabbath and talked to others who do, I have noticed that, although the practices vary, they have some things in common. Different people practice Sabbath differently, but no matter how it is practiced, Sabbath allows us to rest, to reconnect with our faith and each other, and to revise the very order of our lives. It invites us to pause, to play, and to pray.

Each of these six aspects of Sabbath—resting, reconnecting, revising, pausing, playing, praying—offers the antidote or cure for the symptoms of our hurried, adrenaline-overloaded, task-oriented culture. This book will examine each in detail.

living in Sabbath Simplicity

Over the past several years, I have been moving toward what I call Sabbath Simplicity: a sanely paced, God-focused life. Sometimes it seems I am making progress, and other times, as I said, I'm a stressed-out soccer mom. My work, the travel it requires, the kids' activities, the demands of my husband's career—all of these seem to conspire to keep us from the joy of Sabbath rest.

But little by little, I'm getting better at stopping. At resting. And at accepting the grace just to do what I can and know that only God is perfect. Sabbath-keeping is a journey, a process. I'm learning as I go along. Just taking time to wonder why I have to *work* at resting is a huge step. I'm finding that if I unplug regularly, I get more done, because my energy and enthusiasm are renewed by rest. I've found power, paradoxically, in unplugging.

How, exactly, do we do that? In today's hectic society, people of all faiths, and even of no faith at all, are longing to take a break. Most think of rest as a luxury, but it's actually necessary for optimum mental, physical, and spiritual health. Those who have learned to take regular breaks to recover are actually stronger and more efficient.

I first explored the idea of Sabbath Simplicity in my book *Breathe: Creating Space for God in a Hectic Life*. Living a Sabbath Simplicity lifestyle is not impossible, nor is there only one way to do it. But by spending time with Jesus (which for me is the focus of Sabbath), I can rest and receive love that isn't dependent upon my accomplishments or efforts. And since writing that book, I've learned more about Sabbath. I still am on the journey, but I thought perhaps some of what I've learned would be helpful to others. I want to give you the gift of Sabbath-keeping, which has been a life-giving practice for me, one I know will bring you closer to the heart of God.

A final note before we get started. In these pages, I will share our story, as well as the stories of a few other families. I wrote this book over a period of two years or so, often leaving it on the shelf for months at a time. So in various stories, my children will be different ages. They are now eleven and thirteen, but by the time the book is published, they'll be yet another year older. Bear with the discrepancies, which give testimony to the truth that Sabbath Simplicity is a journey, not a destination.

1

shaking things up

What Jesus Said about Sabbath

Do not think that I have come to abolish the Law or the Prophets;
I have not come to abolish them but to fulfill them.
—Jesus (Matt. 5:17)

What did Jesus teach about the Sabbath? Something shifted tremendously in how people followed God after Jesus walked our planet. Although the roots of the Christian faith are in Judaism, the way that modern Christians keep Sabbath, or don't, looks quite different from the way ancient Jews did. Jesus said he came not to abolish the law but to fulfill it. But really, that fulfillment changed a lot about how people lived out their faith.

Why? We have the same Old Testament Scriptures. Jesus, it seems, created this seismic shift that affected how God's law would be lived out. Sabbath is not the only law that was affected, but that's where we'll focus for now.

a new yoke

Even when Jesus walked the earth, people were aware that he was shaking things up. The gospel writers often tell us that people marveled at Jesus' teaching because he spoke with "authority."

Commenting on the rabbinic tradition and this idea of authority, pastor and author Rob Bell writes, "Different rabbis had different sets of rules, which were really different lists of what they forbade and what they permitted. A rabbi's set of rules and lists, which was really that rabbi's interpretation of how to live the Torah, was called that rabbi's yoke. When you followed a certain rabbi, you were following him because you believed that rabbi's set of interpretations were the closest to what God intended through the Scriptures. And when you followed that rabbi, you were taking up that rabbi's yoke."[1]

Bell continues, "Most rabbis taught the yoke of a rabbi who had come before them.... Every once in a while, a rabbi would come along who was teaching a new yoke, a new way of interpreting the Torah. This was rare and extraordinary.... Now imagine if a rabbi who had a new perspective on the Torah was coming to town. This rabbi who was making new interpretations of the Torah was said to have authority. The Hebrew word for 'authority' is *shmikah*. This might not even happen in your lifetime. You would hike for miles to hear him. A rabbi who taught with *shmikah* would say things like, 'You have heard it said ..., but I tell you ...' What he was saying is, 'You have heard people interpret that verse this way, but I tell you that this is what God really means in that verse.' "[2]

So Jesus offered this new yoke, which he claimed is easy. But in a way, it seems harder. He often began with "you've heard it said" and cited the Old Testament law. Then he followed with "but I say to you." For example, he said, "You've heard it said, 'Don't commit adultery.' But I say, 'If you look at a woman with lust, you've already slept with her'" (Matt. 5:27–28, my paraphrase). And, "You've heard it said, 'Don't murder.' But if you call someone a fool or hate them, you've killed them" (Matt. 5:21–22).

Jesus was saying that this is what God really means by that verse. His teaching encouraged people to hold to a higher standard than mere legalism but also helped them to realize that keeping the law perfectly is an impossible proposition. Examining ourselves in light of the spirit of the law, rather than the letter, points us to our desperate need for grace. Jesus exhorted his listeners to examine their hearts, their attitudes, as well as their actions. He challenged his listeners to bring outward practice and inner reality into alignment. This again directed his most attentive listeners toward grace, not more careful legalism.

Here's what I've noticed, though. Jesus never used the "you've heard it said, but I say to you" formula to discuss Sabbath. He didn't, for example, say, "You've heard it said, 'Keep the Sabbath holy.' But I say ..." And he definitely never said, "You've heard it said, 'Keep the Sabbath on the seventh day,' but I tell you, 'Switch it to the first day.'"

Why is that? Did he say it and it somehow just didn't get written down? Was his teaching on Sabbath edited out of the biblical record?

Jesus did criticize the Pharisees for piling rules onto the people, burdening them with lists of what they couldn't do, not just on Sabbath but in regard to all sorts of regulations and man-made traditions. He accused them of valuing their traditions over the law, saying, "You nullify the word of God for the sake of your tradition," and quoted Isaiah 29:3 to condemn them (see Matt. 15:1–20).

He handed out insults to Pharisees and scribes alike, saying, "You experts in the law, woe to you, because you load people down with burdens they can hardly carry, and you yourselves will not lift one finger to help them" (Luke 11:46).

While he didn't use his "you've heard it said, but I say" formula to teach about Sabbath, he did find all sorts of teachable moments to instruct his followers, and his critics, about Sabbath. Usually this happened when he defended his choices to heal people, cast out demons, or engage in other questionable activities on the Sabbath. Not surprisingly, he focused on aligning our hearts with our actions.

He did say, "The Sabbath was made for people, not people for the Sabbath." And he claimed to be the Lord of the Sabbath. But what does that mean? Does it set us free only from the ceremonial aspects of the law, or from the law entirely?

The thing Jesus seemed to get in trouble for most was breaking the Sabbath, at least in the eyes of the legalists of his day. They watched him closely, seemingly in hopes he would slip up and break the rules, although he hardly seemed interested in hiding his actions from them. In fact, he tried over and over to teach them about the heart of Sabbath, asking, "Don't you on the Sabbath untie your donkey and let him have a drink, or pull your sheep out of a pit?" to point out that compassion is never against God's rules (see Luke 13:15; Matt. 12:11).

Norman Wirzba writes, "Jesus does not obliterate Sabbath teaching but reframes it so that we can see once again, with renewed emphasis, what creation's ultimate meaning is."[3]

Jesus came to die for us, but also to live for us, to show us how to live. He modeled spiritual practices like solitude, prayer, and compassion. If you are someone's disciple, you try to emulate them, try to live as they would. And Jesus kept Sabbath. Not in the way his culture expected, perhaps. He exercised great freedom. If we are his disciples, we will take on his yoke. We will live in this life-giving rhythm of work and rest. Jesus kept Sabbath in a new way, a way that shook things up. As his disciples, we can keep Sabbath too. And apparently we're free to shake things up as well.

Jesus shakes things up

In just the first three chapters of Mark's gospel, we find three Sabbath stories. Two take place in the synagogue, one out in a field. Without using the words "you've heard it said, but I say," Jesus still manages to teach a new way of looking at Sabbath.

Let's look at the first passage.

> They went to Capernaum, and when the Sabbath came, Jesus went into the synagogue and began to teach. The people were amazed at his teaching, because he taught them as one who had authority, not as the teachers of the law. Just then a man in their synagogue who was possessed by an evil spirit cried out, "What do you want with us, Jesus of Nazareth? Have you come to destroy us? I know who you are—the Holy One of God!"
>
> "Be quiet!" said Jesus sternly. "Come out of him!" The evil spirit shook the man violently and came out of him with a shriek.
>
> The people were all so amazed that they asked each other, "What is this? A new teaching—and with authority! He even gives orders to evil spirits and they obey him." News about him spread quickly over the whole region of Galilee.
>
> As soon as they left the synagogue, they went with James and John to the home of Simon and Andrew. Simon's mother-in-law was in bed with a fever, and they immediately told Jesus about her. So he went to her, took her hand and helped her up. The fever left her and she began to wait on them.
>
> That evening after sunset the people brought to Jesus all

the sick and demon-possessed. The whole town gathered at
the door, and Jesus healed many who had various diseases.
He also drove out many demons, but he would not let the
demons speak because they knew who he was.

—Mark 1:21–34

Okay, so what did Jesus' Sabbath look like? He taught at
synagogue and cast out a demon. But what were the people
more amazed by? It would seem that his teaching was just as
amazing as the trick of casting out the demon. Again, the people
are amazed by his *shmikah*, his authority. He spoke without foot-
notes to a people hungry for truth. Perhaps the encounter with
the demon was just his way of getting rid of a distraction so that
he could continue teaching. But for the people, it was further
evidence of that authority.

But what did the rest of Jesus' Sabbath look like? What did
he do? After services, he went over to Simon's house. Simon's
mother-in-law was sick, but Jesus healed her. The next sentence
says she began to "wait on them," or as the King James Version
says, she began "to minister to them."

In the Greek, the word is *diakoneo*, which can mean "to serve
a meal" but also means "to minister." It's the same word used
to describe the ministry done by a deacon in the church, and
the same word used in Matthew 4:11 when, after Jesus' time of
tempting in the wilderness, angels came and "ministered" to
him. So perhaps Simon's mother-in-law helped her daughter
and the other women prepare a meal, but the original text does
not appear to mean that she waited on them hand and foot all
day. Rather, she was restored so that she could fully participate
in the ministry of community in her home. She was free to be
an active member of the body, to enjoy the fellowship that Jesus
and his disciples shared.

The next paragraph begins, "That evening after sunset." The

Sabbath ended at sunset. But between the healing of Peter's mother-in-law and sunset, there is a time gap in the text. So what happened between lunch and sunset? What did Jesus do then? My guess is that he rested. Maybe he took a nap. Maybe he just enjoyed talking with his disciples or with the women of the house. (Since Simon had a mother-in-law, we can safely assume he had a wife, although she's not mentioned.) The text doesn't say, but is it possible that on that afternoon, Jesus hung out with his friends? That Jesus just rested, in the context of community?

Jesus came to earth to show us a way to live. He taught us how to pray, how to love, how to forgive — by doing it. And in this passage and others, he taught us how to spend time with friends, to enjoy gifts like a good meal and friendship. He modeled Sabbath rest.

Lord of the Sabbath

Just a few pages later, we find the other two Sabbath stories, which again point us to Jesus' radical revision of the Sabbath code. It's interesting that Mark puts these two stories, which seem to happen on two different days, back-to-back in his narrative.

> One Sabbath Jesus was going through the grain fields, and as his disciples walked along, they began to pick some heads of grain. The Pharisees said to him, "Look, why are they doing what is unlawful on the Sabbath?"
>
> He answered, "Have you never read what David did when he and his companions were hungry and in need? In the days of Abiathar the high priest, he entered the house of God and ate the consecrated bread, which is lawful only for priests to eat. And he also gave some to his companions."

Then he said to them, "The Sabbath was made for people, not people for the Sabbath. So the Son of Man is Lord even of the Sabbath."

—Mark 2:23–28

Another time Jesus went into the synagogue, and a man with a shriveled hand was there. Some of them were looking for a reason to accuse Jesus, so they watched him closely to see if he would heal him on the Sabbath. Jesus said to the man with the shriveled hand, "Stand up in front of everyone."

Then Jesus asked them, "Which is lawful on the Sabbath: to do good or to do evil, to save life or to kill?" But they remained silent.

He looked around at them in anger and, deeply distressed at their stubborn hearts, said to the man, "Stretch out your hand." He stretched it out, and his hand was completely restored. Then the Pharisees went out and began to plot with the Herodians how they might kill Jesus.

—Mark 3:1–6

Jesus, being a rabbi, would teach in the synagogue in Capernaum, his hometown. Inevitably, people who needed healing would show up. And Jesus would heal them, and then the Pharisees would get so mad they'd huddle in a corner, like robed mafia leaders, to talk about how they could take Jesus out.

Those Pharisees were schooled in the Scriptures, so much so that they had much or all of the Hebrew Torah (the first five books of what we know as the Old Testament) committed to memory—chapter and verse. So sometimes Jesus alluded to Old Testament Scriptures, perhaps doing that "you've heard it said, but I say" thing in a more subtle way. Even the words that Jesus used to heal the man do this. He could have said, "Be healed," or whatever. Instead he said, "Stretch out your hand."

The Deuteronomy version of the fourth commandment gives freedom as the reason for keeping Sabbath: "Remember that you were slaves in Egypt and that the LORD your God brought you out of there with a mighty hand and an outstretched arm" (Deut. 5:15).

I wonder if Jesus intended this man's "outstretched arm" and his now "mighty hand" to remind the Pharisees of something.

Why did the Pharisees want to kill Jesus? Because he violated Sabbath laws? Because they felt threatened by his popularity? Did they plot against him because he claimed to be the Messiah but didn't match their preconceptions of a messiah? Was it because they thought his interpretation of Scripture was wrong? Because he exposed their hypocrisy? Whatever the reason, everywhere he went, the Pharisees seemed to show up, looking for ways to accuse him.

You'd expect them to be in the synagogue, but in a field when Jesus and his friends are just walking along? Doesn't that seem odd? Didn't they have anything better to do, especially on Sabbath? Like ... rest? Why were they out stalking Jesus that day? Didn't that violate Sabbath too?

Could it be that Jesus didn't have to say "you've heard it said" about the Sabbath because he simply showed people a radically different approach to Sabbath-keeping? So radical, in fact, that religious people wanted to kill him?

What was Jesus saying with his actions, his infuriating, confusing actions? Even when confronted for, say, healing someone, he answered in riddles: if you have an ox, he said, don't you untie him and give him a drink of water on the Sabbath? (See Luke 13:15.) Healing someone, he said, is just untying them from what has held them in bondage. He pointed people back beyond the traditions and rules to the heart of God. He asked them to revise their thinking on what it means to obey God.

Here's what Jesus seemed to be saying with his actions:

"You've heard it said to keep the Sabbath holy, which you've done by avoiding certain tasks. But I say to you, 'Keep the Sabbath by engaging in relationship, by restoring people to community, to wholeness, by setting people free.'"

In John 5, Jesus got even more assertive about being the Lord of the Sabbath. When religious leaders asked why he was working on the Sabbath, he said, basically, it was because he is God. He went to the pool at Bethesda, where he healed a man on the Sabbath.

> So, because Jesus was doing these things on the Sabbath, the Jewish leaders began to persecute him. In his defense Jesus said to them, "My Father is always at his work to this very day, and I too am working." For this reason they tried all the more to kill him; not only was he breaking the Sabbath, but he was even calling God his own Father, making himself equal with God.
>
> Jesus gave them this answer: "Very truly I tell you, the Son can do nothing by himself; he can do only what he sees his Father doing, because whatever the Father does the Son also does. For the Father loves the Son and shows him all he does. Yes, and he will show him even greater works than these, so that you will be amazed. For just as the Father raises the dead and gives them life, even so the Son gives life to whom he is pleased to give it. Moreover, the Father judges no one, but has entrusted all judgment to the Son, that all may honor the Son just as they honor the Father. Whoever does not honor the Son does not honor the Father, who sent him.
>
> "Very truly I tell you, whoever hears my word and believes him who sent me has eternal life and will not be judged but has crossed over from death to life."
>
> —John 5:16–24

Jesus claimed to be equal with God; he claimed to be the

Messiah. The religious leaders were furious. He also claimed to be above the law, saying that he could work on the Sabbath because God never stopped working, and that he too could do as God did. No wonder the Pharisees got a bit angry.

As he did with all of Jewish traditional law, Jesus changed the outward expression of Sabbath but did not change its inner spirit, its purpose, which is to point us toward God. Jesus often healed people on the Sabbath, confounding the legalists of his day. Surely healing constituted work, didn't it? But those afflicted with disease not only suffered the pain of their infirmity but were disconnected from community. The man with the withered hand, the woman who was bent over, any number of others who received his healing touch—all were isolated. Considered to be unclean, they could not participate in the life of the synagogue. No one would touch them, because to do so rendered a person unclean as well. Jesus restored their physical health not just to alleviate their pain but to restore them to community, which was a way of restoring them spiritually. And it is this spiritual reconnection and restoration that Sabbath practice provides.

For Jesus, Sabbath provided an opportunity to heal, to restore, to renew, to invite those who'd been left out back into the kingdom. He described his mission on earth with these words: "The Spirit of the Lord is on me, because he has anointed me to proclaim good news to the poor. He has sent me to proclaim freedom for the prisoners and recovery of sight for the blind, to set the oppressed free, to proclaim the year of the Lord's favor" (Luke 4:18–19).

What holds you in bondage? Are you a slave to your to-do list? Are you imprisoned by your schedule? Have your activities and busyness become your taskmaster? Are you longing for freedom?

In his Sabbath actions and teachings, Jesus fulfilled this

mission of bringing freedom. And he proclaimed that the kingdom of God is not just for rule-keepers. He flung open the gates of heaven, demonstrating a radical inclusiveness. That is the heart of Sabbath. It is a gift for all people, if only we would choose to receive it.

2

resting

A Release from Our Restlessness

*We are every day becoming aware of the costs of a life without rest.
Increasingly, social workers, courts and probation officers
are raising our children, rescuing them
from the unintentional wasteland of our hyperactivity.*
—**Wayne Muller,** *Sabbath: Restoring the Sacred Rhythm of Rest*

I have always been a bit of a restless soul. Impatient, tempted to live in the future rather than in the present, I'm forever thinking that if I can just get this contract or finish this project, if I can just get through the school year or get through the summer, then things will either really get going or finally settle down—or both.

The illusion I labor under is that when things really get going or finally settle down, I'll be able to focus on what matters. I'll be content. I'll live a simple and serene life.

In my pursuit of contentment and serenity, ironically, I often feel as if I'm running like crazy but getting just about nowhere. I think, "I need to do something," but I can't always tell what it is. My default response to this crisis is simply to get busier. I think to myself, I'll just make a list, accomplish a task, work more hours, or, if I get desperate enough, try to clean up and organize my house (which I'm not very good at, which leaves me feeling even more overwhelmed).

They say insanity is when you keep doing the same thing over and over, expecting different results. So if running like crazy equals getting nowhere, then it's a little crazy to think that more running could ever equal getting *some*where. To get somewhere instead of nowhere, I need to change the first half of the equation. I need to stop.

Stop? What's that? Stop? Is that possible? I can't do that. I wouldn't get anything done. I wouldn't have any accomplishments to point to. What would I say when people ask me, "How are you?" I would feel just a little guilty about lying with the standard answer, "Busy."

Sabbath invites us to stop and to rest. To leave the "unintentional wasteland of our hyperactivity," if only for a while. To be content, even if things are not exactly as we'd hoped they'd be. There is power in stopping, especially for restless souls like me. I don't mean stopping and never going again. That would make life pretty boring. But running without stopping also depletes life of meaning. To pause between the notes of our lives turns noise into music. It's called resting. It's the antidote for restlessness, but one we don't think of. When we feel restless, we often think, "I've got to do something." We rarely think, "I've got to do *nothing*." But therein lies the beautiful paradox of Sabbath rest. As the Tao Te Ching says, "Who is it that can make the muddy water clear? But if allowed to remain still, it will gradually become clear of itself." To practice Sabbath is to practice a stillness that brings clarity to our lives.

So many people tense up when I mention Sabbath to them. They frown, worried I will come at them with rules, a legalistic approach. Or they laugh, in a "yeah, right" type of way. As if *that* could happen, they say.

Others tell me how Sabbath-keeping has shaped their families and their hearts. I hear stories about how God meets them in a place of rest. I hear stories about children who get to enjoy their parents, moms who get a break from their endless chores, families who reconnect over the dinner table or on a bike ride. While the results—greater joy, deeper relationships—are often the same, the methods of Sabbath-keeping vary widely. There are no rules, except this: just stop.

So rather than rules, I'll offer guidelines for stopping. I'm inviting you to discover the freedom in rest, the serenity that living in Sabbath Simplicity offers. I'm inviting you to consider receiving the gift of God's rest.

What does it mean to rest? How, exactly, do you recover your life when you aren't even sure where or how you lost it in the first place? Why, in our accomplishment-driven, 24/7 society, would you want to rest? What's the point?

As the quote at the beginning of this chapter points out, our restlessness injures the people around us, who need our attention more than they need our accomplishments. Our children need us to have the time to look them in the eyes, to ask about their lives, to give them the gift of attention. And we need that as well.

Resting seems wasteful, extravagant, a luxury a person as busy as we are cannot afford. But really, and here's another paradox, resting is as necessary as breathing if we are to do more than cling to the cliff of life by our fingertips. It's something we cannot afford to do without but, once we learn how to do it, feels luxurious. It's a gift, but we can't receive it if we don't stop to open it. Once we do, we realize that stopping, resting, is actually the secret to getting more done, to understanding and living our true priorities, to enjoying our lives, and to experiencing the presence of God.

a rest from consuming

Our culture labels people as consumers, as those who consume things, buy things. We are defined, at least in part, by our possessions and are profiled by our buying patterns. We don't just *look* differently at a man who drives a new Mercedes than one who drives a rusted-out Ford; we judge the *value* of those two men differently as well. Companies spend countless dollars to monitor our brand choices. They know which kind of salad dressing we buy and how much we spend a month on entertainment, but they know nothing of our souls.

And as a result, many of us don't know ourselves at a soul level either.

When we aren't consuming, who are we? If we stop, just for a short time, so that we are, even for a day, not a consumer, then what do we become? For some of us, that's a scary question. It's what keeps us scurrying, even if we don't realize it. If we rest from shopping, buying, or even writing a shopping list, we reject the idea, if only for a while, that we are what we buy. If we rest from our work, from endless meetings and tasks, we reject the idea, if only for a day, that our value lies in our accomplishments. We may say that we know these things are not true, that we know we are not defined by possessions or accomplishments, that it's what's inside that matters, but do we live it? How do we spend our time? Our money? Our energy?

Stopping gives us a great gift, especially if in that stopping, we respond to this divine invitation: come to me. We get a chance to be our true selves—fully loved children of God who share that love with others. We realize that we are beloved lovers.

Such awareness cannot come if we refuse to stop. Of course, in a culture that values going, doing, accomplishing, consuming, that's easier said than done. Still, regular rest will make us more efficient and more joyful. It's in real rest—spiritual rest—that we recover our true selves, rediscover our joy. Who wouldn't want such a gift?

In spiritual rest, we recover our lives. We discover the gift of community with people and with our Creator, and the depth, texture, and richness that gift adds to our lives. We get a chance to stop, turn, and really notice the faces of the people running through life beside us and to feel grateful for them. This is no small gift.

I think we often don't take a break because we think we won't be able to get everything done. But we're tired, so even when we are working, we're halfhearted about it. We are never fully engaged, and we never take time to disengage. We're neither running nor stopping; we're wandering, feeling lost.

To run without stopping violates God's design. Study after study of human efficiency shows workers get more done if they take breaks than if they don't. This is true not just in factories but in families as well. Optimum function is a result of both effort and rest. But we are more than machines. We need rest not just for efficiency's sake but for soul healing.

When we rest from consuming, we are free from the lie—which we say we don't believe, even though we live as if we believe it with all our hearts—that things will make us happy. When we rest, for a day or just for a few moments, we are free to love and to notice the needs of others, needs which often are not material but spiritual. And in a divine paradox, when we meet others' spiritual needs, our own are mystically and supernaturally met as well. When we give of ourselves to meet spiritual needs—for love, for friendship, for someone just to listen—we are replenished. We recover our deepest life, the heart of who we are. We say, "I am not a consumer. I am a lover."

a day apart

The Bible tells us to keep the Sabbath "holy." At its heart, holy does not mean religious. It means different, set apart. That which is holy is sacred, the opposite of mundane. To keep Sabbath means to set aside one day of the week to rest.

Our calendar says the day officially begins during the night—at midnight. In our daily lives, we reckon the day's beginning somewhere around sunrise, about 6:00 a.m. for most of us (except for teenagers, who, if they ran the world, would begin the day somewhere in the vicinity of noon).

But in the biblical tradition, the day begins not at sunrise but at sunset. We see this in the creation story in Genesis, where, starting with verse 5, we hear, "And there was evening, and there was morning—the first day." This refrain repeats a few verses later, "And there was evening, and there was morning—the second day," and so on, all the way to the sixth day.

By the seventh day, the Bible says, God was done. God had finished the work of creation, so he stopped. And Sabbath-keeping calls us to remember the work of God and also to stop. To call the day holy, different, set apart.

So Sabbath begins not with waking but with resting. It begins at sunset the night before. We gather with family or friends for a meal or to hang out, and we go to sleep. The first and best part of the day is relationship and rest. When people ask, "How can I *do* Sabbath?" I ask them, "Do you know how to eat, relax, and sleep? If so, you've 'done' almost half a Sabbath."

The thing is, many of us don't even know how to do that, or we think that to do so every week would be self-indulgent.

We grab food quickly from the drive-through. We don't talk to the people we live with. We sit beside them staring at a screen, getting to know people we'll never meet—the characters in television shows—while missing out on everything the people on the couch beside us have to offer. We know more about the characters on our favorite television shows than we do about our friends, which led Robert Putnam, in his social commentary *Bowling Alone*, to observe that more people watch *Friends* on television than have them.

We lie awake at night, wondering why we can't sleep or what life is really about. Countless ads on that little screen tell us we can get a good night's sleep if we just take a certain pill, so we do. But sometimes, before the sleeping pill kicks in, we think, "There has got to be a better way. There has to be more to life than this."

what's missing?

Just as our muscles need to work and then rest in order to get stronger, our souls need to be challenged and then recover in order to grow. Just being alive in the twenty-first century is challenging. It's the recovery part we don't know how to do, and it is slowly killing us. "We live in a world that celebrates work and activity, ignores renewal and recovery, and fails to recognize that both are necessary for sustained high performance," write Jim Loehr and Tony Schwartz.[1]

Loehr and Schwartz are performance experts. They help athletes and corporate leaders improve their performance by learning how to be what they term "fully engaged." They write, "At the most practical level, our capacity to be fully engaged depends on our ability to periodically disengage."[2]

Loehr, a performance psychologist, evaluated top-ranked tennis players in an effort to determine what makes those who hold the highest world rankings better than their lower-ranked competitors. What do they do as they play tennis that makes them superior players in a highly competitive sport?

Here's what one of Loehr's colleagues writes about the study: "To his growing frustration, he [Loehr] could detect almost no significant differences in their competitive habits during points [in a tennis match]. It was only when he began to notice what they did *between* points that he suddenly saw a difference. While most of them were not aware of it, the best players had each built almost exactly the same set of routines between points.... It dawned on Jim that these players were instinctively using the time between points to maximize their recovery."[3]

Top performers, Loehr discovered, know when to work hard and when to rest. They create routines (sometimes without realizing it) that allow them to recover even between points. Their strength lies not in the perfection of their strokes or their level of effort but rather in their ability to recover. To get stronger, an athlete must push past his or her current limits, but then—and this is critical—they must rest and allow their muscles to recover. During the time of rest after exertion, muscles grow in size and strength. And the same is true mentally. The top tennis players, Loehr discovered, find rituals (the way they walk, breathing patterns, self-talk) that lower their heart rate, calming them and, in effect, allowing them to rest both physically and mentally between points. And the rest and recovery, even in the thirty seconds between points in a tennis game, is what makes all the difference between players who win the most and those who don't perform as well.

Loehr and Schwartz took what they learned from sports performance and created a "Corporate Athlete" system for improving performance on the job and in all areas of life, which is detailed in their book *The Power of Full Engagement*.

But what if you're not a world-class athlete or a CEO? What

if you are just an ordinary person? What if you're like me, a mom who's trying to take care of her family, volunteer at church and the kids' school, stay healthy, nurture her spirituality, stay connected with her friends, and, oh yeah, have a career as well?

No matter what job we do, all of us would like to do well. I don't know anyone who wakes up and says, "I sure hope today is boring." We may feel resigned or sad because we are depressed or burned out, but few of us would say we aspire to mediocrity.

God designed us to love and appreciate excellence, so we find deep satisfaction in doing our best. Think about how amazed you are by a beautiful work of art or music or even something spectacular in creation. Beauty woos our souls. But most of us go about trying to do our best simply by trying really hard, by running without stopping. And the truth is, we're not really at our best. We're just tired. We say our schedule is demanding, but the schedule isn't the one barking orders. It's our attempts to demand too much from a day, more than a day is meant to give. We are the ones who are demanding, but our tyranny ultimately is against our own souls.

Recovery is the key to full engagement, to peak performance, whether you are leading a Fortune 500 company or a family of five, whether you are an athlete or an office worker. And in order to recover, we have to stop. We have to rest. It's important not just for physical fitness but also in the mental, emotional, and spiritual areas of our lives.

recover your life

I love Jesus' invitation to all people: "Are you tired? Worn out? Burned out on religion? Come to me. Get away with me and you'll recover your life. I'll show you how to take a real rest" (Matt. 11:28 MSG).

What does it mean to "recover your life"? Jesus offers us a "real rest," which goes deeper than a bit of time when we "just chill." Jesus says, "Just come to me and find deep soul rest." He doesn't necessarily ask us to become more religious. Rather, he invites us to "get away" from religious activity if it is not helpful, if it's burning us out.

In my own life, I want to learn how to take a real rest. Why? Not just because it would be nice or I'd be happier. I believe God has called me to his purposes, to do certain things, like be a good mom to my kids, write books and articles that help people live more meaningful lives, love the people he's placed in my life, be compassionate to those less fortunate than myself, and be mindful and kind. If I want that kind of life, then I need to figure out a way to live it. To respond to God's calling on my life, I must give my best effort. That doesn't mean I run without stopping. Neither does it mean that I do things halfheartedly, conserving my energy.

If I never fully expend my energy and never fully rest either, I'll never increase my capacity. Like an athlete, I have to sometimes push myself. How? I have to forgive when I think I can't; I must choose to act lovingly even when it's hard. By acting lovingly, I become more loving. But then I also need times when I simply rest, times to withdraw from people and their demands, times when I allow myself to spend time with Jesus, to take him up on his invitation to "come with me by yourselves to a quiet place and get some rest" (Mark 6:31). In those moments of what I call "sacred selfishness," I let Jesus attend to my deepest needs: for quiet, for peace, for intimacy with him.

Sabbath-keeping helps us recover our lives. It's what is missing from our hectic, hurried lives. It's the missing part of the rhythm that God designed us to live in.

To grow as a person, to experience a deeper spirituality, to grow closer to Jesus, I must find a rhythm of life that includes times of full engagement, balanced with times of complete and soul-satisfying rest. Is that even possible? What would that look like in your life?

one woman's story

Sometimes, Sabbath-keeping truly is as simple as just resting.

Letitia Suk works as a speaker, writer, and life coach. She and her husband, Tom, live in the suburbs of Chicago. Her focus for Sabbath is to "spend the day in life-giving pursuits." Her practice has looked different in various seasons of her life.

Her children, now in their twenties, are out of the house, but she's been practicing Sabbath for many years. When her children were still living at home, she modified her practice in certain ways. For example, she'd do her grocery shopping very early Sunday morning, when the store wasn't crowded. But after church, she'd come home and relax. "It was harder with Sunday kids' activities like sports," she admits. "But I am very intentional about having a change of rhythm from the rest of the week and allowing time for rest."

Her Sundays now begin with a quiet time with God. "Before church I might read a part of an inspirational book in addition to my usual quiet-time reading," she says.

She and her husband go to church, but after that, it's a day to cocoon at home, at least for her. "I put comfortable clothes on. Once I get in the door, I rarely go out again. I read the Sunday paper, take a nap, maybe put a few photos in an album, cook something if I'm in the mood. Later in the afternoon, my husband and I will have a planning meeting to talk about finances or schedule, but that is life-giving, not a chore. In the evening we will watch a fun TV show or sometimes rent a movie. The 'being home and not going out' theme is important to me, so even going out to a movie feels like too much going out. We have other evenings to do that. Occasionally the topic at the Sunday night service seems compelling enough to go, but it has to fit the 'life-giving' criteria."

That same standard applies even to socializing, which means she usually doesn't socialize on Sundays, except with her adult children. She does nothing to advance her career, either. She says, "I do no writing, coaching, or speaking preparation. No returning phone calls or business emails. I have considered shutting off the computer but do enjoy 'fun' emailing, so I will do that."

Letitia's work as a life coach requires intense interaction with other people, and so her Sabbath provides soul-balancing solitude. "I look forward to it and know I can hang on till Sunday regardless of how busy the week is," she says. "The spillover from the rest and change of rhythm carries me to midweek, when I can start looking forward to it again! I truly feel rested in mind and body."

Being an empty nester makes Sabbath easier to practice in some ways. But it's okay to adapt to your season of life. "Our four children are on their own (mostly), and my husband also enjoys the pace of Sabbath, but he is more flexible about it," she says. "He might go to a meeting about something that interests him or go to the gym and work out. He doesn't seem to need the 'staying home' part of the day that is so valuable to me. He certainly respects my observance."

What can we learn from Letitia's story? She's using the day to take care of herself, to rest. Her husband joins in at times, but she is not waiting for him to take the lead in their practice. She's adapted her practice over time, as her season of life has changed. In certain seasons, her Sabbath rest lasted only part of the day on Sunday. Perhaps you cannot practice Sabbath in exactly the way she does. But what can you learn from her pattern of rest? Which parts of it could you include?

While it may seem like Letitia is doing very little, her rest enables her to return to her work on Monday with renewed strength and energy.

rest brings strength

My husband, Scot, loves to sail. He's been racing sailboats since age seven. He actually proposed to me on the boat, after we had sailed in a race together. (He prayed fervently the whole race that we wouldn't tip over, because he had hidden the ring *in the boat*.)

However, I was not the regular crew in his twenty-foot two-man scow. So the first year of our marriage, I sat in a motorboat and took endless photos of sailboat races, worked on my tan, and basically was bored out of my mind. I'd sailed with him occasionally and realized that scow racing is a fun but physically demanding sport requiring balance, quick thinking, and also a lot of physical strength. Having grown up horseback riding and water-skiing and running, I had good balance, felt comfortable on the water, and considered myself quite fit. I'd sailed with Scot several times, including a few races. I could handle it, or so I thought.

So I offered to help Scot by joining him on the boat as his crew. He and his sailing buddies were skeptical. I think some even said something along the lines of "you can't have your *wife* sail with you," implying that my gender might be, for this sport, a liability. At the time, only men raced in this fleet. Obviously these boys didn't know me very well, and Scot didn't either, because if they did, they would have known that anytime anyone ever told me "girls don't ..." or "girls can't ..." that automatically inspired me to prove them wrong. I may have said something along the lines of "just watch me."

Since having more weight on the boat (as ballast) is critical to sailing, and because physical strength is essential to the task of crewing, Scot told me I could sail with him, but only if I hit the gym. And gained about ten pounds. That's right, here was a newlywed telling his slender bride to pack on some pounds. Of course, it had to be muscle. I think he figured this would dissuade me. Nope.

Scot, who in college had briefly aspired to be a professional bodybuilder, devised a workout regimen that would, he said, help me "bulk up for summer." Great. We already belonged to a health club where I had dabbled in yoga and aerobics classes and played around on the Nautilus machines. You know, sort of girly-girl exercises. But Scot led me to the back of the gym, where the free weights were kept. Large-armed men and intimidating women with sweat-stained leather belts around their waists grunted in front of a mirror as they threw huge iron weights around. We were definitely not in the Jane Fonda workout room anymore.

According to my husband/personal trainer, I would do "pushing" exercises three days a week and "pulling" exercises the other three days. Pushing exercises included various types of bench presses, push-ups, triceps extensions, and leg presses. Pulling exercises included lat pull-downs, biceps curls, leg curls, and sit-ups. On the days that I did pushing exercises, the pulling muscles got to rest and recover. And vice versa for the other days.

I would use weight heavy enough to do only about five or six repetitions in a set, and do three sets of each exercise, my Arnold Schwarzenegger wannabe husband explained. Because the weights were heavy, by the last rep in each set, I would be almost in "muscle failure," which was, he said, the goal.

"I want my muscles to fail?" I asked.

"When you work to failure, the muscle fibers actually break down," he said, in what sounded like an Austrian accent. "Then when you rest, blood flows into the muscles and they rebuild themselves." I waited, expecting him to say something like, "We're here to pump you up!" Thankfully, he didn't.

Okay. Resting between sets and between workouts was actually just as important as the weight lifting. Got it. That I could do. But rest without exertion would not build anything except flab. The rhythm of fully engaging, followed by full rest, would bring about the results I wanted. Neither one alone was enough.

It only took me a few months to get a much stronger back and arms. (Remember, I was motivated to defend the competence of women athletes—indeed, women—everywhere.) Muscle weighs more than fat, so I gained about six or seven pounds without adding too much bulk. My biceps got a bit bigger, but my pants still fit; in fact, they fit a bit looser, since all this exercise toned up my waist a bit.

How did I increase my physical strength and endurance? Not by just sitting around thinking about it. Not by overtraining, working out constantly and obsessively. If I wanted to increase my strength, I needed to put forth full effort, and then rest. The key: fully engage my muscles and push them to the limit. And then, rest them. The rest was just as important as the work.

The next summer, I sailed with Scot. Let's just say we surprised his friends with how well we did. I've now been crewing for fifteen years, and it's been a fun way for us to spend time together, and a strong incentive to work out.

What's true in the physical realm is true in other areas of life. Many of us, though, spend a lot of time meandering. We never really work out mentally or spiritually, but we never really rest, either.

daily rest

Loehr's discovery about how tennis players rest between points in a tennis match brings up another important point: we need to rest more often than just once a week.

God made our bodies to need sleep. When we sleep, our

bodies rejuvenate themselves. Often, when we are sick, we need extra sleep, because sleep helps our bodies heal. In our society, many of us have become so used to hurrying, we see sleep as an inconvenience or an indulgence of the weak. We brag about being able to manage on only a few hours of sleep.

Sleep is a gift, a little healing miracle every night. Like the gift of Sabbath, most Americans reject that gift or find that they are working so hard that they are too keyed up to sleep well.

The 2007 National Sleep Foundation's *Sleep in America* report focused on women specifically because they are more likely than men to have sleep problems. The poll found that more than half of American women (60 percent) say they get a good night's sleep only a few nights per week or less, and 67 percent say they frequently experience a sleep problem. Additionally, 43 percent say that daytime sleepiness interferes with their daily activities. A similar report in the early 1990s estimated that seventy million Americans suffer from some sort of sleep disorder.[4]

God designed us. He designed the planet we live on. Each twenty-four-hour day is divided roughly in half between a time of light and a time when it is dark. Obviously, this shifts a bit during the seasons—winter's days are quite short where I live. Even so, God's perfect design allows us to work and play and get things done during the light, and to rest and sleep when it gets dark.

We've created our own world, though, in which we work and keep busy far into the night. Overriding our natural rhythms enables us to get more done, but it's also the reason so many of us struggle with sleep disorders.

God made our bodies in an amazing way. From a physiological standpoint, here's what happens: "When working properly, our bodies respond to nature's cues to create their ideal rhythms. For example, when functioning properly, the human circadian rhythm will respond to the morning light of a new day. This light will cue the body to produce cortisol, serotonin, and other hormones and neurotransmitters that get a person awake and going and cause blood pressure to increase and body temperature to rise. At sunset, the body receives another of nature's cues and responds to dusk and ultimately the night's darkness. As the sun goes down the body will produce and secrete the hormone melatonin, and blood pressure will drop as the body prepares for and eventually falls off to sleep."[5]

When it is light out, we are awake. When it gets dark, the systems God created in our bodies, circadian rhythms, slow us down. The problem is we don't stop when the sun goes down. We have electric light, which is a wonderful convenience, but we use it to extend our workday far into the night. Some of us work shifts that are outside of the natural rhythm, and while we can adjust, it's not easy. According to the National Sleep Foundation, "before Thomas Edison's invention of the light bulb, people slept an average of ten hours a night. By 2002, Americans were averaging a little less than seven hours of sleep on weeknights and 7.5 hours per night on weekends."[6]

Sometimes we override our body's natural rhythms with stimulants, like caffeine. But we also have a chemical in our bodies, adrenaline, which gives us a boost of energy. God designed it for use in emergencies only. In fact, it's called the stress hormone. But we tend to abuse it, and many of our stress and sleep problems stem from the fact that our bodies are overloaded with adrenaline to the point that we can't shut down. When we work too much, we're exhausted, but because we're working too much and messing with the normal cycles of our bodies, we can't sleep.

One of the primary causes of sleep disorders is stress. And increasingly, rather than taking steps to dial down the stress in their lives, people are simply turning to medication. A study released in 2007 by Medco Health Solutions, Inc., a pharmacy-benefit management company, says that Americans' use of sleep medications rose dramatically between 2001 and 2006. It's not just adults who are turning to pills to help them sleep. Medco's study says that "use of prescription sleep medications by children under age 19 surged 45 percent between 2001 and 2006; and 52 percent among adults age 20 and older. Growth in use of the medications among seniors age 65 and older increased 26 percent over the five-year analysis period."[7] Children and teens are taking sleep medicines? Are they having sleep problems or just watching too many Ambien commercials?

In his book *Making Room for Life*, author and pastor Randy Frazee points out that when we live at a crazy pace, we not only have health problems related to our lack of sleep, but we also lose connectedness with others. Randy writes, "The impetus for my initial search for connectedness or community was not a need to prepare a sermon or write a book but a need for personal sanity. I knew I couldn't obtain connectedness by increasing my speed or extending my hours of work."[8]

Randy is a pastor at my church, and I've had the privilege of working with him when we were both speakers at a conference. Randy's quest for connection and for sanity came when, after years of working too much, he found he could not sleep. He'd prided himself on being able to work long hours and get by on only a few hours of sleep. But after a while, his body rebelled against that abuse. He really could not sleep at all. His doctor (whom he saw only after forty-five days of not sleeping!) told him he had so flooded his body with adrenaline that he simply would not be able to get back to normal sleep cycles without medication unless he drastically changed his lifestyle.

To find a sane rhythm of work and rest, Randy looked to Scripture, where God showed him a rhythm of life that he and his family adopted, which he calls "the Hebrew Day Planner." He writes, "There are essentially three major activities in each day that should be governed by night and day: *productivity*, *relationships*, and *sleep*. Because the work of the Hebrew was agrarian, productivity was accomplished during the hours of sunlight—6:00 a.m. to 6:00 p.m. At 6:00 p.m. the sun would set and darkness would begin to descend. From that point on, the time would be devoted to relationships—time with the family, extended family and friends; sharing a meal; and a time of storytelling (no TV or Internet).... The basic structure of a normal day for the Hebrews went like this: twelve hours available for productivity and work (6:00 a.m.–6:00 p.m.); four hours available for relationships (6:00 a.m.–10:00 p.m.); and eight hours available for sleep (10:00 p.m.–6:00 a.m.)."[9]

We need rest on a daily basis, and even during our day, we need to take breaks to stop, breathe, and connect with God and the people around us. How can we practice Sabbath? We have to begin by learning to live at a sane pace each day.

In order to live according to this Hebrew Day Planner, Randy and his wife, Rozanne, made radical changes in their lifestyle. They decided to replace their children's activities with family time. They had dinner together each night. Since he couldn't go back to work (as had been his habit previously), Randy tried to figure out ways to stretch those family dinners from their typical fifteen-minute time frame. He asked the kids questions about their day, in great detail. After dinner (which eventually stretched into an hour-long family time), they continued to spend time together. When they lived in Texas, they sat out in their front yard. Amazingly (or not) they began to get to know their neighbors and found their sense of disconnection and isolation began to melt away.

In my own life, living in this rhythm is not easy. I write six days a week. Monday through Friday, while the children are at school, I start early—by 7:00 a.m., which is when they walk out the door. I sometimes take a break somewhere in my day to exercise. I stop when the kids get home, to talk to them. When they begin their homework, I get back on the computer for an hour or two. I try to stop around five, when I begin my "second shift" of meal prep, housework, laundry, and helping kids with homework. The schedule is flexible, which is great, but also challenging. I often find myself answering emails after the kids are in bed. Saturdays I spend some of the morning writing (while others sleep in), but I also tackle housework in the afternoon, to prepare for Sabbath. Often the kids need me to drive them somewhere.

Now, the sun is setting, a bit before 5:00 p.m. (It's November.) I'll stop writing until tomorrow and go prepare a meal for my family and spend some time with them—and also get a few household chores done. Thankfully, soccer season is over, so our evening may include some time to help the kids with their homework, hang out and talk, or even play a board game. Last night, we invited a friend whose wife is out of town to share supper with us.

During soccer season, I am sometimes driving a car pool in the evening hours. Because my kids are in only one activity each and we are part of a car pool so I don't have to do all the driving, I don't have to live in my car. But carpooling can be a relationship-building time. As kids get older, they may not want to talk to their parents as much as they used to. But sometimes they'll open up, in the safety of the car, where they are behind you or beside you. Not having to look you in the eye, they feel a bit safer.

If you are the type who keeps running all the time, perhaps the first step on your Sabbath Simplicity journey is to begin to see the evening as a time to take a small rest, to reconnect relationally, to stop. It's not easy, especially if you work outside the home, but again, focus on progress, not perfection.

finding a real rest

"We build emotional, mental, and spiritual capacity in pre-cisely the same way that we build physical capacity," Loehr and Schwartz write. "We grow at all levels by expending energy beyond our ordinary limits and recovering."[10]

What have you done lately to expend energy beyond your normal limits, from an emotional or spiritual standpoint? In the fall of 2005, my friend Deb got on a church bus headed for Waveland, Mississippi, with a group of other volunteers who wanted to do something to help the victims of Hurricane Katrina. The trip stretched her physically, mentally, emotionally, and spiritually. She saw miraculous answers to prayer, such as trucks showing up early in the morning with the food or supplies they'd run out of the night before. Some days tested her emotional strength—for example, the time she had to step between a white woman and an African American woman who were about to come to blows in the supply tent. She worked all day in the stifling heat and slept on a cot in a tent at night. When she wasn't working in the "store" where hurricane victims could select free supplies, she logged on to her laptop to update a blog about the relief effort for the church website. She engaged fully: physically, mentally, emotionally, and spiritually.

When she got home, she found she needed to rest. Stretching herself strengthened her, but taking time to rest and reflect on the experience brought even deeper insights, nurturing new growth in her soul. It boosted her confidence and also her faith.

If we want to grow, to become a stronger person, to become a more spiritual person, we must seek experiences that stretch us. Maybe we need to get on a bus to Waveland, or just walk over to a neighbor's house with a meal and a willingness to listen for a little while. And then make sure we take some time, as

Psalm 46 says, to "be still and know." In resting after spiritual work, we realize that even when we do good, we are not God.

If we want to get stronger mentally, we will have to engage with something a little weightier than, say, Nick at Night or *People* magazine. Or if we have a job that requires a lot of mental energy, we'll need to find ways (other than magazines or television) to truly give our minds a rest.

As a working mom, I sometimes feel I never have a moment to myself. But I also need to ask, Do my kids have a moment of my time when I am fully engaged with them? Or are they always on my heels, asking for what I don't want to give them—and not getting it because I am "busy"? When my daughter was young, she would say, "I need some Mommy and Melanie time," time when I fully engaged with her, even if we simply played a game, colored together, read a story, or snuggled.

As a gift to yourself, try this: next time someone asks for your time, put aside whatever multitasking you are doing and just be fully engaged with them for five minutes. Look them in the eye, really listen. Somewhere else in your day, get out of the house or close your bedroom door and be alone and rest for five minutes. Fully disengage. What if you lived every day like this, alternating full engagement with rest or disengagement?

It's possible to rest in one area of your life while engaging in another. For example, my job sometimes requires me to sit at a computer, to think and write. I expend a lot of mental energy. But typing isn't exactly a physical workout. Another part of my job involves speaking to groups of people, which for me takes tremendous emotional energy. Since I am often writing and speaking about spiritual topics, I find that my work is spiritually challenging as well.

So when I am working at my computer, I am at rest, physically speaking, but I am fully engaged mentally and, at times, emotionally and spiritually as well. To rest mentally, I engage in physical activities, such as walking the dog, playing tennis, and sailing. When Scot and I sail, we take a break from the mental and emotional challenges of our work. We unplug, literally, since you can't bring your laptop or cell phone on the boat.

Our increased ability to stay in touch via cordless technology makes it harder to unplug. Even on vacation we feel compelled to check email and voice mail, so that we never really get a complete rest. We're not working, but we're not really resting, either. Or we're so bent on having fun that our vacations exhaust us.

And the fact is, in order to do our best when we are working (whether our work is mothering or manufacturing), we need to just rest everything. We need to stop.

Simply sitting in the back yard listening to the birds is restful for me both mentally and physically. Looking at the trees or the stars feeds not only my mind but my soul. What's restful to you? Have you ever even considered the question? Do you make time for rest—not just sleeping but relaxing, preferably somewhere besides in front of the television?

If we want to grow spiritually, we need to find ways to challenge ourselves. Perhaps by learning to meditate on Scripture, filling our minds with its truth, even committing it to memory. Maybe by spending time alone, in silence and solitude. Or by volunteering to do something that will challenge our limits for compassion, such as serving the poor or going on a mission trip. Or choosing to forgive someone who has hurt us.

practical help

Henri Nouwen writes that a spiritual discipline is simply creating some space in our lives in which God can act. So the first part of Sabbath as a spiritual discipline is simply to create the space for it—to clear our schedules and put aside our worries without concern about how to "do the practice." This is easier said than done. To create some space, we will have to learn to say no to opportunities that sound good, no to putting our kids or ourselves into too many activities, no to overscheduling.

For many of us, family is the place where we rest, the context in which we can be most authentic. But sometimes family is a source of stress. Consider the possibility that some of your family stress may be the result of overscheduling and not just because the people you live with are difficult.

If you are single or an empty nester, you may have to expand your thinking about what constitutes family. In certain seasons of life, your "family" may be your roommates or a circle of close friends. They may or may not live under the same roof, but they know you and care for you.

Maybe you are lonely: you believe people who care are scarce. But a scarcity mindset never brings us closer to God's abundance. Maybe that's why you keep yourself so busy and why you never rest. Because rest would feel lonely. Which is exactly why rest is so important. In resting, you experience the abundant grace of God, a lavish gift never earned, only received. His presence relieves our soul loneliness in a way that no one and no thing ever could.

Nouwen also writes that the rest of solitude is an essential first step toward community. Paradoxically, time alone with God enables us to engage with people. Solitude imbued with God's presence not only fills us; it softens us. It makes our hard shells permeable so we can give and receive love. "When you discover your belovedness by God, you see the belovedness of other people and call that forth. Solitude is where spiritual ministry begins," Nouwen writes. "Community is not loneliness grabbing onto loneliness: 'I'm so lonely, and you're so lonely.'

It's solitude grabbing onto solitude: 'I am the beloved; you are the beloved; together we can build a home.' "[11]

That's what family is: people who know, because of their individual experience of God, that they are loved. They know it so well that they can see it in others and can share with others out of their abundant supply of love (provided by God). So if you are lonely and looking for family, what you really want is love. But only divine love will satisfy. If we can seek God, rather than grasping at others to meet needs only God can meet, we will be filled with that love and offer it to others. Love is found in rest, in a time of simply being with God. And it's shared in community.

Poet Rainer Maria Rilke writes, "Love … consists in this, that two solitudes protect and border and salute each other."[12]

Still, Sabbath is meant to be a time of community. We gather with other Christians to worship God together. It is a day of resting, not just alone but with our family and friends.

one mom's story

One mom who responded to a blog discussion on Sabbath said she and her husband and children keep things simple on Sabbath. Because they are part of a church that meets on Saturday morning, they practice Sabbath from Friday evening to Saturday evening. This mom writes, "Sabbath in our home starts early in the week as we prepare all week long. I spread out the housecleaning, so by Friday afternoon the house is all clean with minimal stress. We start our Sabbath celebration with a special meal on Friday night—usually fruit and French bread—Wal-Mart has wonderful bakery French bread for only a dollar a loaf! We often will light candles and play relaxing music to set a special ambience. We take out special toys for the kids, too, that they get to play with only on Sabbath. We'll read to the kids, watch them play, read ourselves, and just enjoy being together. I will often take a soak in the tub. We all head to bed on the early side. Sabbath morning we sleep in a little bit and then enjoy breakfast together before heading to our church's early service."

What principles can we take away from this simple story? First, you don't have to spend a lot of money, but you do have to spend some time getting ready. Just as you would prepare to have a guest in your home by doing errands and chores before they arrive, you have to do some work ahead of time to simply enjoy God on Sabbath. By cleaning the house the day or two before Sabbath, by stocking the pantry so you don't have to shop, you set yourself free to rest on Sabbath.

Second, small touches can create a restful atmosphere, and again, they don't require us to spend a lot of money. They do require intentionality. A simple, inexpensive, but special meal marks the day as different. Hiding a few special toys away during the week and taking them out only on Sabbath, lighting a candle, putting on music reserved for Sabbath (at our house it's Mozart) all create an atmosphere that says, "This day is special; it's different. Holy. Set apart."

Third, it's a day of simply connecting with family—simply by talking, playing together, reading, going for a walk. If you have small children, reading to them is a great Sabbath practice. Having Daddy read is even better, because statistics show that fathers often spend less time with their children than mothers do. Children need to hear their father's voice, and reading is a great opportunity for that. Mom can help pick the book, if needed. It can be the Bible or a Christian book, but it doesn't have to be. It can be a good children's story that adults can enjoy.

Sabbath is a day when this mom gives herself permission for a leisurely soak in the tub, a day when they get the children and themselves to bed early. What if your Sabbath journey were to begin with a commitment to getting enough sleep (eight or more hours) one night a week? If you normally get less than eight hours of sleep, this might be a good place to start.

While rest does help us become more efficient and helps us maintain stronger health, it is not enough motivation, I think. Most people know that eating properly and exercising will make them stronger and healthier, but that doesn't mean they do it.

We rest not just to be healthy but because God told us to do so. It's a commandment so many of us see as outdated or irrelevant. We've lost touch with the roots of our faith, the context of the commandment. Without that context, the law becomes meaningless. While we may keep Sabbath in a way that is different from God's people in the ancient world, we can still learn much from understanding the heart behind God's commands. In the next chapter, we'll take a look at the law and see how this "ancient-future" practice is relevant to our lives today.

3

reconnecting

A Rescue from Isolation

Judaism tries to foster the vision of life as a pilgrimage
to the seventh day; the longing for the Sabbath all days
of the week which is a form of longing
for the eternal Sabbath all the days of our life.

—Abraham Joshua Heschel,
The Sabbath: Its Meaning for Modern Man

As Friday afternoon slips into evening, the smell of a brisket, cooked slowly, fills the house, which has been thoroughly and lovingly cleaned, as if in preparation for an honored guest. Rae and Herb Lowe are in the kitchen, putting the finishing touches on the meal. Their best dishes and crystal stemware have been lovingly arranged on a cream tablecloth embroidered with the six-point Magen David, the star (or more accurately, the shield) of David. An ornate kiddush cup, sterling silver overlaid with gold, sits on a saucer. Two loaves of challah, traditional braided bread, studded with sweet raisins, wait patiently in a basket.

On this evening, as is often the case, several of the couple's grown children and grandchildren gather around the dining room table. The family recites a passage from the Torah, from Isaiah 58. "If you call the Sabbath a delight and the LORD's holy day honorable ..." (v. 13).

After the Scripture, they sing a simple Shabbat shalom melody and say a prayer of thanksgiving.

Then Rae stands and places a scarf over her head and speaks a traditional prayer. As the woman of the house, it is her duty to welcome the Sabbath.

"Lord of the Universe, I am about to perform the sacred duty of kindling the lights in honor of the Sabbath," she begins. After her prayer, she lights two candles. She gently cups her hands around the flame and fans the smoke toward herself three times. As darkness falls outside, the family gathers in the candlelight.

Rae sits down and together the family prays the Shalom Aleichem, then recites a psalm.

Herb stands and places his hands on his sons and says a blessing on them, then on his daughters, then finally on his grandchildren. Then he turns and blesses Rae with words from Proverbs 31, a chapter of the Torah that speaks about a wife of noble character. At this point, the family sometimes strays slightly from tradition, allowing the grandchildren and children to bless their parents and each other as well.

Herb then pours wine into the ornate pewter kiddush fountain, made in Jerusalem. "You place the kiddush cup on a saucer, because when you pour it, you always overflow the cup," he explains. "It's a rich symbol—the blessings of God cannot be contained. Wine is a symbol of joy—the joy of the Lord can't be contained."

All gathered at the festive table take a drink of the wine after Herb has blessed it by praying, "Blessed art thou, O Lord our God, King of the Universe, who creates the fruit of the vine."

After the wine comes a prayer to sanctify the Sabbath, followed by a blessing over the bread, which is passed around the table. The two loaves provide a remembrance of the time of the Hebrew exodus, when God provided manna, bread from heaven, for the children of Israel. On the day before the Sabbath, they were told to gather double portions, because God would not work on the Sabbath.

"All week I look forward to the Sabbath," Herb says. "You're remembering the last one, but you are anticipating the next Shabbat. It's a day of rest, a day to focus on each other and on God."

Believe it or not, the Lowe family is not Jewish. But they have rediscovered the roots of their Christian faith in Judaism, and with it, the joy of Sabbath-keeping. They first began learning about the Jewish foundation of Christianity after being invited to a seder feast back in the mid-1970s, when they were attending a Lutheran church. But they added the traditional Sabbath dinner and practice to their weekly routine only about six or seven years ago. This ritual has become a spiritual practice, a way of creating some sacred space in their week where God shows up. It provides a way to connect spiritually with friends and with each other.

The Lowes attend an Anglican church, but they often visit other churches to share what they've learned about Judaism and its relationship with Christianity, and to encourage other Christians to celebrate what they say are not just Jewish feasts but the Lord's feasts. "If you're going to effect change, you need to do it from inside," Herb says of his efforts to get Christians to embrace the whole of their faith heritage.

Rae says she and her husband feel God has called them to minister to the church, to invite Christians to reconnect with their Jewish roots. "We're no longer aliens," she says. "We've been grafted in. He's coming back for one bride, not a harem.

Christianity is not a separate tree but a branch grafted onto the people of God."

They have studied under top Jewish scholars to learn more about the faith tradition that Jesus himself grew up in. They consider themselves to be Christians, followers of Jesus, but wanted to know more about Jesus' Judaism, his culture, and how it influenced Christianity.

Their Sabbath looks more like the Hebrew Shabbat, celebrated with traditional prayers and a traditional meal. As is the Jewish custom, their celebration begins on Friday evening and ends at sunset the next day—the seventh day, Herb points out, the day that God himself rested after creating the world.

"We've made a conscious decision to stop going the way of the world," Herb says. "I believe that's the heart of Jesus, to fulfill the promises of God. Our goal is not just to be Sabbath-keepers but to help others look at Jesus, to teach what God has mandated."

"It is to our own detriment that we ignore God's feasts," his wife adds. "We're too busy."

Connecting with their Jewish roots, connecting their faith to the ceremonies and traditions that Jesus himself engaged in, has brought deeper meaning and joy to their lives. "God honors a heart that's willing to honor him," Herb says. "That's the heart of Shabbat shalom."

the heart behind the command

It seems odd that God would need to command rest. Wouldn't people want to take a break after working? In our culture, we tend to be too hurried, too busy, because we are deeply committed to a belief in our own importance. We're afraid of taking a break, perhaps because we are afraid the world might stop spinning if we get off the treadmill.

But the children of Israel may have had the opposite problem. They didn't know how valued they were. They didn't think they were allowed the luxury of a day off, because for years in captivity, they had not been allowed that. That's why Sabbath was such a gift, but also a command. They'd been slaves who never had a day off.

God knows that about us: that we tend to think too highly of ourselves, that we tend to think our value lies in our accomplishments. That we believe way too much in our indispensability. That we make ourselves God. Or that we wrestle with a different demon altogether. We believe too firmly in our unworthiness. We think our hard work keeps God's love flowing our way. We think we are not good enough, that we have to keep earning the approval of someone—God, our parents, our peers. Either way, we end up serving the false god of our own competence.

But to worship there is to cage our own souls, rejecting the freedom Jesus purchased for us. When we think we cannot afford to take a break, we leave unopened the amazing gift of God's rest. We put ourselves back into the slavery Sabbath intends to free us from. Pastor and author Mark Buchanan writes, "To refuse Sabbath is in effect to spurn the gift of freedom. It is to resume willingly what we once cried out for God to deliver us from. It is choosing what once we shunned."[1]

Such a distorted view of our efforts and busyness, ironically, does not make us feel connected to others in a meaningful way. Rather, it exacerbates our isolation.

We live in a time when communications technology is incredibly advanced. We can email, voice-mail, text-message, instant-message, or, if need be, even talk face-to-face. We have computers, cell phones, PDAs, MP3s, GPSs, and so on. Yet despite our advanced communications systems, we live in a time of increasing loneliness and isolation. We often feel disconnected.

God's heart behind any of his commands is love. And God's love is the antidote for our feelings of disconnection and purposelessness. Sabbath provides connection with God and others. The Sabbath commandment flows out of God's desire to connect with us, to ease the ache in our hearts with sheer presence. If we dare to obey, Sabbath allows us to do a little experiment, to test the promises of God: what if I stop working, stop accomplishing, stop earning? Will God still love me? Will he love me just as much?

Of course, the answer is that he won't love us any less. Because nothing will ever change God's love for us. Taking a day of rest allows us to experience that truth in a concrete way, to live into the truth we say we believe but perhaps might not fully embrace. While nothing can make God love us more, when we rest we perhaps experience his love more deeply, because we become more keenly aware of the unconditional nature of that love. Keeping Sabbath, we can "taste and see that the Lord is good; blessed are those who take refuge in him" (Ps. 34:8).

common roots

In my work, in my neighborhood, and even at church, I encounter many people who seem to feel disconnected, isolated. They have issues with their family, like everyone. They don't like their coworkers or their boss. They didn't grow up in a church, but now they are exploring faith in a nontraditional setting. Or they grew up going through the motions of a religion they did not understand and have moved away from that and think they have found something completely new and different, but they don't realize that what they now embrace is just another branch on the same tree.

I am not saying all denominations or religions are the same—not at all. But the Christian faith has its roots in Judaism. Understanding and embracing that, as the Lowes have done, will make our lives more meaningful. Herb and Rae are quick to point out that they have not converted to Judaism, that they are not Messianic Jews (people born into the Jewish faith who choose to follow Christ, believing he is the Messiah). Rather, they have embraced "the Lord's festivals" and believe that the Lord of the Old Testament is the God of both Judaism and Christianity. Like their Jewish forebears, Christians worship the God of Abraham, Isaac, and Jacob. Understanding and embracing our spiritual heritage, we find the connection and community we long for. And a huge part of that heritage is found in the pages of Scripture, including the Old Testament.

The cure for our isolation and disconnection is not simply more relationships but deeper ones, and a deep connection to our shared past. We can embrace new things but treasure and value tradition.

silver and gold

When I was a little girl, I joined Brownies, the first step in Girl Scouting. Ugly brown and orange uniforms aside, I loved Brownies, especially because my mom and our neighbor, Mrs. Merritt, were our troop leaders. We sang songs, earned badges, created useful projects such as a "sit-upon"—a piece of oil-cloth folded over itself, stuffed with newspaper or foam, and stitched closed with yarn—designed, of course, for "sitting upon" the ground, around the campfire. (Brownies are big into campfires.)

We sang a song in Brownies, usually as a round. (Brownies are big into singing rounds.) "Make new friends, but keep the old," it went. "One is silver and the other's gold." I remember asking, "Which is gold?" and my wise mother saying, "Which do you think is gold? Which is more valuable?" Those with whom we have a shared past are precious in our lives.

Here's the thing: we have, with all believers and even with those of the Jewish faith, a shared past. We may not all believe the same things or agree. Sadly, though Jesus prayed that we would be one, we're divided into thousands of Christian denominations, and even within Judaism there are different groups (Reformed, Orthodox, etc.).

But in keeping Sabbath, we connect with our common roots; we connect with something bigger than ourselves to find that the Lord truly is Lord of all. We find the gold of a shared past, of traditions. And we, by affirming that connection, anticipate with our lives the day that "every knee shall bow and every tongue will confess that Jesus Christ is Lord," when the Lord of the Sabbath will gather his people in unity.

Because of our culture's infatuation with progress and the future, we sometimes forget the lessons of history, to our detriment. But beyond our roots in Judaism, we have centuries of tradition within the Christian church. In the first few centuries after Christ's death, early church fathers wanted to distance themselves from Jewish practices and traditions, including the rituals and rules of Sabbath. They saw their faith in Christ as a new beginning, and that in his death, Christ had "abolished" the ceremonial law, which included Sabbath-keeping. Instead, they focused on what some referred to as "the eighth day" (implying a whole new beginning) or the first day of the week as "the Lord's Day," which was focused on gathering for worship, communion, and teaching, rather than simply a day of rest. In fact, some early Christians criticized Jews who rested on the Sabbath as lazy and idle. Ignatius wrote that Christians should observe the Lord's Day as a festival, and that the day before, Sabbath, should be spent in meditation on God's Word rather than focused on rituals of a meal and rest. But for many centuries, many Christians observed both days.

Through the centuries, various cultures and denominations practiced Sabbath differently. Luther and Calvin had different opinions. People in various parts of Europe, especially during the Reformation of the 1520s, practiced Sabbath differently. The English were much tighter than the French, for example. Many of the Christians who came to be known as Separatists or Puritans were in favor of stricter restrictions on what could or could not be done on Sabbath, and they argued that by rising from the dead on a Sunday, Christ instituted that day of the week as the true Sabbath. Finding resistance to their religious practice in their native England, the Puritans immigrated to the Netherlands, a place known for religious freedom and tolerance. They eventually found that tolerance, however, a bit too lax.

While our deepest Christian roots are in Judaism, most American Protestant Christians also have roots in the Puritan movement. A huge factor in the Pilgrims' move to the Netherlands, and from there to the Americas, was their desire to practice their religion, including very prominently Sabbath, as they believed it should be.

Craig Harline writes, "Puritan exiles often expressed disappointment with how their new Dutch neighbors observed the Sabbath. Everywhere on Sunday were strolling players, jugglers and worldly attire.... Exiled English Puritans grew weary of such attitudes after a couple of decades and began sailing in steady numbers to the New World from 1619 on.... One reason stated repeatedly by the departing English was how little they had been able to reform the Dutch Sabbath around them."[2]

Unfortunately, the Puritan Sabbath became increasingly legalistic. Religious leaders (who were also government leaders) meted out strict punishment for falling asleep in church, wearing clothes that were too ostentatious, and other crimes we might consider odd.

Historian Murray Rothbard writes:

> One Puritan moral imperative was strict observance of the Sabbath: any worldly pleasures indulged in on the Sabbath were a grave offense against both church and state. The General Court was shocked to learn, in the late 1650s, that some people, residents as well as strangers, persisted in "uncivilly walking in the streets and fields" on Sunday, and even traveling from town to town and drinking at inns. And so the General Court duly passed a law prohibiting the crimes of "playing, uncivil walking, drinking, and traveling from town to town" on Sunday. If these criminals could not pay the fine imposed, they were to be whipped....
>
> To enforce the regulations and prevent the crimes, the gates of the towns were closed on Sunday and no one permitted to leave. And if two or more people met accidentally on the street on a Sunday, they were quickly dispersed by the police.... Under the inspiration of the Rev. John Cotton, the New England Sabbath began rigorously at sunset Saturday evening and continued through Sunday night, thus ensuring that no part of the weekend could be spent in enjoyment. Indeed, enjoyment at *any* time, while not legally prohibited, was definitely frowned upon, levity being condemned as "inconsistent with the gravity to be always preserved by a serious Christian."
>
> Kissing one's wife in public on a Sunday was also outlawed. A sea captain, returning home on a Sunday morning from a three-year voyage, was indiscreet enough to kiss his wife on the doorstep. For this he was forced to sit in the stocks for two hours for this "lewd and unseemly behavior on the Sabbath Day."[3]

Those rules seem almost laughable in our day. Even if we

didn't grow up in such a strict tradition, such pharisaical strictness is part of our collective past. It is, I think, what makes us think Sabbath-keeping equals legalism. This is unfortunate, because legalism is not what God intended. Just look at how Jesus practiced the Sabbath and kept breaking the Pharisees' rules. I think that if Jesus had made an incognito visit to America in the 1600s, he likely would have been put in the stocks or flogged within a few hours of his first Sunday.

Even apart from religion, our culture has a weekly rhythm that includes a weekend off from work, although many of us are busier on weekends than during our workweek. This is also a part of our history and cultural heritage. Tilden Edwards notes, "Labor laws in the United States and elsewhere during the nineteenth century asserted the right of government to protect laborers from the physical and moral debasement of uninterrupted labor. These laws often went further and protected Sunday as a day of shared rest, so that family life and other relationships could be nurtured in a way that would be impossible if days off were staggered."[4]

Half a century ago, stores and businesses were typically closed on Sundays, and churchgoing was considered patriotic. Today, Sunday is a big shopping day. For some stores, it's the busiest day of the week, the only day working women have time to shop.

But is shopping truly relaxing? Especially if you are in debt? By that, I mean that your credit cards are carrying over a balance from month to month, or that you have debt other than one mortgage on your home. Does adding more debt ultimately make you more relaxed? Rather than looking at no shopping as a deprivation, see it as a step toward freedom, the freedom that comes from getting out of debt.

As you explore what it means to keep Sabbath, it's worth looking at the ways various cultures and denominations have lived it out in the past. What gold can you find in traditions and ancient practices that might bring you farther along on your Sabbath journey?

Sabbath freedom

In the Old Testament laws, given by God to his people, the children of Israel, God offers a guide for right living, rules that really are in our best interests. The moral code set the Israelites apart from the world around them. The laws were not capricious, and it soon became clear that following God's way actually led to freedom, health, and joy.

The Sabbath command is woven throughout the stories and laws of the Old Testament. While Genesis does not mention the word Sabbath, it does point out that God rested or, more accurately, "ceased" his work on the seventh day.

Jesus followed these laws in his own life but taught that following them was not a matter of legalism but of having a heart toward God. His standards were much higher than most people expected. For example, as we noted in chapter 1, he taught that if you even look at a person with lust in your heart, you've broken God's commandment forbidding adultery (Matt. 5:27–28). In our sexually charged, porn-soaked culture, that's not an easy path for many people. But it is the way that leads to life and freedom. And Jesus continually communicated freedom—not freedom to go your own way but freedom to relate to God through the intimacy of grace.

The Old Testament laws are not the means of our salvation. That comes only by grace, by the free gift of Jesus' sacrifice for us on the cross. But God's law shows us how to follow Jesus and how to live according to what Jesus proclaimed to be the most important law of all: to love God and love others.

Even the Ten Commandments focus on these two precepts. The first three direct us toward loving God: don't worship other gods, don't make idols to worship, don't take God's name in vain. The last six are about loving others: honor your parents, and don't murder, commit adultery, steal, lie, or covet.

Even if we are tempted to worship other gods, like the god of our comfort or the god of money, we know it's wrong. When our casual idolatry of wanting more stuff is pointed out to us, we agree, in theory at least, that "godliness with contentment is great gain." Most of us would agree that lying, killing, adultery, and so forth are harmful, not only to others but ultimately to us.

But the fourth commandment, to keep the Sabbath, trips us up. We don't see it as a moral issue, but there it is in the midst of a code of moral conduct that has shaped all of Western civilization. Although I must admit the influence of the Ten Commandments is waning and even being resisted in some cases.

The Sabbath command, though, is not an anomaly. It is the hinge, the piece upon which all the other commandments hang, for it is about both loving God and loving others. It provides a segue between the God-focused and the others-focused commandments.

"The seventh day is a sabbath to the LORD your God," Exodus 20:10 says, and it is, first and foremost, a day focused on God. But God doesn't stop there. To love God is to love others without prejudice. For then comes the list of those who shall rest: all people. The Sabbath command is a hierarchy-flattening one: the rich do not rest at the expense of the poor. No one is excluded from the right to put aside their work and to rest in the presence of God. Men, women, children, slaves, even animals are provided for by the grace of God.

The Bible contains two lists of the Ten Commandments, one in the book of Exodus and the second in the book of Deuteronomy. (Deuteronomy comes from the Greek name *Dueteronomion*, which means the "second law," because it reiterates the content of previous books.)

Most commands are pretty straightforward, so God does not elaborate but simply commands: don't worship idols, don't lie, don't kill, don't steal. They reflect God's values: truth, life, respect, contentment. But the Sabbath command is different. God offers specifics: don't just you rest but everyone in your house, even slaves and animals. Additionally, God gives a reason for the command. "Keep the Sabbath because . . ."

Interestingly, the reason is different in each list. In Exodus, Sabbath is about remembering creation—God rested on the seventh day, so the people of God should rest on that day as well. As Dorothy Bass writes, this is a command given by the God who not only created the big wide world but also made us, small and made of dust, but image-bearers nonetheless. God knows us and how we can function optimally: "Our bodies move to a rhythm of work and rest that follows the rhythm originally strummed by God on the waters of creation. As God worked, so shall we; as God rested, so shall we. Working and resting, we who are human are in the image of God."[5]

But in Deuteronomy, the reason for observing Sabbath is because God's people were to remember that they had been slaves. "Slaves cannot skip a day of work, but free people can," Bass notes. "To keep Sabbath is to exercise one's freedom, to declare oneself to be neither a tool to be employed—an employee—nor a beast to be burdened. To keep Sabbath is also to remember one's freedom and to recall the One from whom that freedom came, the One from whom it still comes."[6] In other words, keep Sabbath because you can, because you are free to do so, which is no small gift.

Remembering our past slavery also reminds us to have compassion on others who are enslaved, on those who have less than we do. Many of the world's poor today live in actual or virtual slavery. But ceasing our endless consumption and acquisition, we remember those who do not have enough, who are not fully free because of their economic status.

You may feel like a slave at work, working for an unreasonable taskmaster. You may face huge pressures not just to accomplish tasks but because you know you could easily be replaced if you slack off. And you need your job. You can't just quit. If that's your situation, you deeply need Sabbath, at least one day of freedom. You need a day to remember that even though your job is difficult, the truest thing about you is that you are a child of God, that you are free.

In Luke, we read about Jesus healing a woman who had been crippled. Luke tells us "she was bent over and could not straighten up at all" (13:11). To heal her, what does Jesus say? "Woman, you are set free from your infirmity" (13:12). Interesting word choice, especially since he healed on the Sabbath. When the religious leaders protest, Jesus responds that Satan has kept the woman bound, but he sets her free on the Sabbath day.

In our culture, we sometimes think of freedom as individualistic. To us, freedom is individual autonomy. But that's not the kind of freedom Jesus gave this woman or that Sabbath gives us.

Because of her illness, this woman was looked down on, excluded. Considered unclean or at least avoided. Jesus set her free, free to be a part of community. Sabbath freedom offers us a chance not to go our own way but to be healed and restored to community, to straighten up and praise God with others. Jesus saw healing on Sabbath as a worthwhile activity because by healing, he restored relationships.

In my previous book, *Breathe*, I point out, "It's been said that the fourth commandment is the only one Christians like to brag about breaking. Why? I think, whether we are ministers or mothers, clerks or CEOs, we believe that if we are busy, we must be important. To honor the Sabbath does not mean to run at mach speed for six days, then collapse in a trembling pile of adrenaline-wasted uselessness on Sunday—only to get up and run the rat race again the next day."[7]

That lie, that if we are busy, we must be important, is what drives much of our frantic activity. The Sabbath command reminds us of our value but also warns us not to put our faith in our accomplishments. The two different versions of this command remind us that we are made in the image of God, yet we were slaves to sin. God delivers us and shows us how to live. Both reasons point us toward loving God and remembering that we are not God.

The two commands also differ slightly in another way. In Exodus, God's people are told to remember (*zachor*) the Sabbath. But in Deuteronomy, the injunctive is to observe (*shamor*) the Sabbath. Observant Jews make note of the distinction and incorporate both commands into their Sabbath practice. Because we share with the Jewish faith a reverence for the Scriptures, it is worth exploring these two words and their significance.

remember

We live in a culture that values the future more than the past. Phrases like "that's so yesterday" or even "that's so five minutes ago" point to our fascination with whatever is next, new, hot, trendy. Unfortunately, our quick disposal of the past has consequences. By discarding tradition, we cut ourselves off from meaning and significance. By ignoring history, we are exposed to the danger of repeating its mistakes. Our expressions of faith may seem to bloom or even bear fruit for a while, but eventually they can become empty and dead, like a branch cut off from a tree.

Jesus said, "Behold, I am making all things new," but he also told us to remember him, specifically with wine and bread. The communion meal and the Sabbath meal are inextricably linked, because the roots of the communion sacrament are found in a Jewish Shabbat meal of special significance — the Passover seder.

The Bible says we are to remember the Sabbath. What does that mean? Many things, perhaps, but it is partly a call to remember the purpose, the meaning. Because purpose and meaning bring joy. Sabbath is a gift, a source of joy. When Sabbath becomes a day of empty ritual or legalistic rules, our joy disappears, and with it, our motivation to continue to practice it.

Tracey R. Rich, a writer who is a practicing Jew, notes, "We are commanded to remember Shabbat, but remembering means much more than merely not forgetting to observe Shabbat. It also means to remember the significance of Shabbat, both as a commemoration of creation and as a commemoration of our freedom from slavery in Egypt."[8]

For Christians, Sabbath is also a remembering of our being set free from sin, which is one reason many Christians celebrate Sabbath on Sunday, the day Jesus rose from the dead.

In the Jewish tradition, the loaves of bread on a Shabbat table are a reminder of the manna God provided in the wilderness. God rained down manna, the bread from heaven, six days a week. He offered food to the Israelites, who wandered, grumbling, in the desert, a no-man's land between slavery and a home in the Promised Land. On the sixth day of the week, the Israelites were commanded to gather a double portion of this mysterious food, which the Bible says "tasted like wafers made with honey" (Exod. 16:31), because on the Sabbath, God would rest and not provide manna.

Each day, they were to gather "enough" for their household. Not as much as they could, but simply enough. God's Word links the concept of "enough" with Sabbath. It is a day to cease striving, affirming our belief in God's providence, defying the gods of consumerism that say we can never have enough.

If the Israelites tried to gather extra portions on any other day of the week, they would awaken the next day to find it spoiled — "it was full of maggots and began to smell" is how the Bible colorfully describes it (Exod. 16:20). But miraculously, the extra gathered on the sixth day did not spoil but remained fresh — God's Sabbath provision. Even before God gave the Israelites the Ten Commandments, the Sabbath was built into the rhythm of their lives, even as a nomadic people fleeing slavery. God had given them the Sabbath, even before he gave them the law.

Always, the Sabbath is a reminder of God's provision. God told his people, "Bear in mind that the LORD has given you the Sabbath; that is why on the sixth day he gives you bread for two days" (Exod. 16:29). If we "bear in mind" something, we *remember* it. This is one reason the traditional Shabbat table has two loaves of challah bread — a tangible, edible reminder of God's gift of extra provision on the sixth day.

Manna foretold, symbolically, the promised Messiah. "I am the bread of life," Jesus told his followers. "I am the living bread that came down from heaven. Whoever eats of this bread will live forever. This bread is my flesh, which I will give for the life of the world" (John 6:35, 51).

Jesus' strange metaphors confused the religious leaders of his day, confounded his own disciples, and can seem strange to us today. But here's what I know: beyond our physical hunger, in a deeper place, we all have hungry souls. We all long for relationships free from mind games and manipulation, second-guessing and score-keeping. And that hunger can be satisfied only in an intimate relationship with Jesus. I know this from my own experience, but also from hearing the stories of others.

A Jewish Sabbath meal ought to feel familiar to Christians because it is set with bread and wine, the elements of the communion table. As well it should. Jesus instituted the practice of communion around a special Sabbath table during the Feast of Passover.

If we don't remember the significance of Sabbath and link it to God's provision for our spiritual ancestors and for us, we'll forget. That seems obvious: if we don't remember, we'll forget. But if we forget the significance of Sabbath, it's easy to let it slide or to let the day morph into something else—a day just to chill out or to focus on ourselves. Sabbath is a day to rest and refresh ourselves, but it is so much more. It is a day to remember. Our remembering creation, deliverance, and salvation points us toward remembering the deep love God has for us.

Mark Buchanan writes, "The Exodus command, with its call to imitation, plays on a hidden irony: we mimic God in order to remember we're not God. In fact, that is a good definition of Sabbath: *imitating God so that we stop trying to be God.*"[9]

We remember that God created the world, including us. We are not God. We remember that our ancient spiritual ancestors were trapped in slavery and that against impossible odds, God delivered them. We remember that we too were slaves to sin, but Jesus set us free with his loving sacrifice.

observe

The Deuteronomy list exhorts us to "observe" the Sabbath. Despite our common ancestry, Jews and Christians differ on what this means. To ask, What does it mean to observe Sabbath? for some of us, anyway, is to ask, What activities are permitted, or not permitted, on Sabbath?

Observant Jews refrain from thirty-nine specific categories of work on the Sabbath. However, the type of work prohibited is *melachah*, which refers not so much to physical labor or even paid employment as to "work that is creative, or that exercises control or dominion over your environment."[10] For example, lighting a fire (or the modern equivalent, turning on a light) or harvesting grain (modern equivalent, shopping) are prohibited. The specific activities prohibited are precisely those activities engaged in to build the tabernacle of God (more on this in a later chapter).

God did this type of work in the creation of the world, which is why the Sabbath command points to creation. The rhythm of creation is melachah and Shabbat—to create and then to stop creating.

Jewish practice says no to melachah but yes to joy. The Bible exhorts us in Isaiah 58 and elsewhere to "call the Sabbath a delight."

For Christians, the "rules" are less restrictive or, for some traditions, just different. Various Christian groups through the centuries have come up with their own lists of Sabbath melachah.

For example, one of the things forbidden on the Jewish Sabbath is handling or using money. So shopping, trading, and so on were forbidden. This was carried on in various cultures throughout history, although in certain periods of history (much to the dismay of religious leaders), Sunday was a day to visit with friends at the tavern, where, certainly, the drinks had to be paid for.

The Puritans, as we mentioned earlier, had strict standards for behavior, opposed any sort of commerce on Sunday, and punished Sabbath-breakers severely. Up until a few decades ago, many stores in the United States were closed on Sundays, and in some regions, "blue laws" prohibiting the sale of certain items (such as liquor or tobacco) remain in effect even today.

Some denominations prohibited work, while others emphasized working for God on the weekends. Dianne, for example, told me that when she was in college, she was involved with an Independent Fundamentalist Baptist church in Chicago. She writes, "Growing up, Sundays were pretty much just another day, although we did go to church. At college, though, they were a nightmare."

Hardly what you'd expect for a day of rest. That sounds about as far from calling the Sabbath a delight as you could get. But her church's evangelistic methods (which apparently were not optional for the college-aged members) meant that Dianne and other church members spent all day Saturday in the inner city recruiting kids for church. The next morning, "We were on buses on Sunday by 5:00 a.m. to go pick those kids up and didn't get a break until we got home from evening church around 9:30 p.m." The schedule was grueling. After college, she worked as a teacher and attended a similar style of church, though, she says, "I think there was time for a nap in the afternoon. I just kind of burned out, and Sundays went back to being just another day."

Years later, Dianne is now exploring, cautiously, what a different sort of Sabbath practice might look like. The churches she attended in the past were demanding in other things, not just service on the Sabbath. She's prayerfully looking for a more balanced approach to her faith.

Another woman told me that when she married into a Baptist family, her mother-in-law chided her for folding laundry (a simple task she found relaxing) on a Sunday. Yet the mother-in-law had no qualms about preparing Sunday dinner or puttering in her garden. (Gardening, this young woman said, would seem like work to her.)

This raises an interesting question: do you practice Sabbath differently than your parents? Has this been a conscious choice, or have you sort of drifted into the Sundays that you now live, driving your children to various games and activities, running errands in between, and wondering, at the end of the day, what happened to your weekend?

In some churches, Sunday can be a busy day when staff and volunteers must work hard to put on a service, care for children, visit the sick, and so forth. If such volunteerism is coerced, the day can feel anything but restful.

Which raises another question: if you feel drawn to the spiritual practice of Sabbath, does the church you attend support you in that? Does it provide a framework for Sabbath rest?

Sometimes in our attempts to shake off the shackles of legalism, we set ourselves so free that we get lost. But finding that place where we are connected to God and to others, yet not weighed down, is not easy. I believe God meant for us to find connection with him in the context of community. Does your church help or hinder your Sabbath-keeping practice?

Ideally, Sabbath is a day when we can focus exclusively on what Jesus said are the most important commandments: to love God and to love others. During the week, I find it difficult to live in the way I wish I could—loving God and loving others. Sabbath is a day to look into the eyes of others, to listen to them, to encourage them, and to spend time with God, loving and receiving love. Ideally, I think, our church is a place where we have the opportunity to learn in community, to talk about what it means to follow Jesus, to encourage others and receive their instruction, encouragement, and love. In other words, to worship God together. That's the heart of Sabbath, right?

But the external practice, what that looks like, is quite flexible for Christians. I spoke to Christians in various denominations, and some (like Seventh-day Adventists) found that their church strongly supported their efforts to practice Sabbath-keeping. But it was easy for those same denominations to slide into legalistic interpretations. Others said their church made it harder for them to take a day of rest, since committee meetings and other obligations were often scheduled for Sunday afternoons. Some churches seemed to be neutral on the subject, leaving individuals to their own devices. But the mere freedom from obligations at church, in a way, wordlessly supports a restful Sabbath.

The question many people wrestle with, or perhaps don't wrestle with enough, is, Do Christians have to practice Sabbath at all? Obviously, various individuals and denominations have differed on this over the years. Each claims to be following what the Bible says, and yet they have come up with different rules and practices.

Rob Bell writes, "Jesus expects his followers to be engaged in the endless process of deciding what it means to actually live the Scriptures." He notes that Acts 15 describes the discussions the early church had about whether Jewish practices (not just Sabbath but others that likely prompted more adamant discussion, like circumcision) needed to be adapted by all followers of Jesus. He notes that this process must always happen in community, but that we are always in the process of figuring out what it means to follow the teachings of the Bible, and that none of us can be completely objective about what the Bible is saying. "When you hear people say they are just going to tell you what the Bible means, it is not true. They are telling you what they *think* it means. They are giving their opinions about the Bible.... And the more that I insist that I am giving you the objective truth of what it really says, the less objective I am actually being."[11]

The early church wrestled with figuring out what the Bible means, especially since they were followers of a rabbi who had told them over and over, "You've heard it said, but I tell you."

Paul, a Jewish follower of Jesus, counseled the church at Colosse, "Therefore do not let anyone judge you by what you eat or drink, or with regard to a religious festival, or a New Moon celebration or a Sabbath day. These are a shadow of the things that were to come; the reality, however, is found in

Christ" (Col. 2:16–17). In other words, figure out, in the context of community, how to practice your faith.

But just because we are no longer bound by the law doesn't mean Jewish practices or other historic interpretations of Sabbath are inherently wrong. The practices of God's people expressed, or at least were meant to express, the people's love for God through their obedience to God.

We do have more freedom to figure out what it means to stop, but we still are commanded to stop, to put aside our unfinished chores, our to-do lists, and our hyperactivity. We are commanded to rest, and in so doing, we discover the rest of God, which we so often seek with our frantic activity but cannot seem to find. As Bell points out, God invites us to figure it out not in isolation but in community. Are you a part of a community that is helping you understand what it means to obey God's commandment to stop and rest?

living counterculturally

In our culture, we're accustomed to having a weekend, and we expect a day off from our regular work at least once a week, even if we fill that day with activity. But weekends as we know them simply didn't exist in ancient Middle Eastern culture. God instituted something new and different when he instituted Sabbath. Taking a day off to focus on God was countercultural when God first commanded it, but for different reasons than it is now.

Jewish writer Tracey Rich writes, "In modern America, we take the five-day work-week so much for granted that we forget what a radical concept a day of rest was in ancient times. The weekly day of rest has no parallel in any other ancient civilization. In ancient times, leisure was for the wealthy and the ruling classes only, never for the serving or laboring classes. In addition, the very idea of rest each week was unimaginable. The Greeks thought Jews were lazy because we insisted on having a 'holiday' every seventh day."[12]

Shabbat means to stop. To stop doing your own thing, whether it's corporate work, entrepreneurial work, or house-work, and focus on God. In a 24/7 world, stopping is counter-cultural. But think about this: what if you actually took some time away from even thinking about work? Could you give yourself that gift? Or more accurately, could you open your heart and hands enough to receive it from God?

Keeping Sabbath is not only about ceasing but also about celebrating. How? By taking the time to do simple things you always say you mean to do but never have time for.

What would happen if you were to take a twenty-four-hour period once a week simply to enjoy all the things that you work so hard to have? One reason we work is to earn money. Even if we love our jobs, we are motivated in part to do them because we get paid. We work hard so we can have the things that money can buy, but often we're so busy we don't have time to enjoy them.

But what if you took God up on his offer to enjoy a day with him? Imagine a day that begins with an evening meal that provides a living picture of the abundance of God. Around the table, you pray and sing songs and recite blessings that remind you of all you've been blessed with and, more important, who provided those blessings. In a Shabbat meal, we ingest the sym-bols of God's goodness and provision.

What a lovely notion, I can hear you saying. It sounds like a great idea, but I am too busy. My life is too crazy. I'm not Jew-ish, so these rules don't apply to me. That's a different religion, and although that Sabbath meal sounds intriguing, it would never work in my real life.

Well, what would work in your real life? To keep running

24/7 until you collapse? Or to do things halfway all the time, instead of fully sometimes and resting other times? I don't know about you, but I've tried living that way, and it just wasn't working for me. I wanted more of God, and I found it in spiritual practices, including Sabbath.

"The rest of God—" writes Mark Buchanan, "the rest God gladly gives so that we might discover that part of God we're missing—is not a reward for finishing. It's not a bonus for work well done. It's sheer gift. It is a stop-work order in the midst of work that's never complete, never polished. Sabbath is not the break we're allotted at the tail end of completing all our tasks and chores, the fulfillment of all our obligations. It's the rest we take smack-dab in the middle of them, without apology, without guilt, and for no better reason than that God told us we could."[13]

which day?

Since we are looking at Jewish tradition, you may wonder why I celebrate Sabbath on Sunday. I invited my newsletter and blog readers to write to me as I worked on this book, and I learned that many of them celebrate Sabbath on Saturday, since it is the seventh day, and, they told me, since that's what the Bible says we should do—keep the seventh day holy.

While some argue for keeping Sabbath on the seventh day, I think we ought to err, at first, on the side of grace. If someone is not practicing Sabbath at all, if they never stop, ever, then the first step would be to convince them of the merits of stopping at all, rather than worrying about which day is proper.

I would offer that it is better to at least try stopping than to give up on Sabbath-keeping because you simply find the day of the week an insurmountable barrier. You can't be anywhere except where you are, as one of my mentors likes to say. So if you are the type of person who never stops except to fall into bed at night, then just setting aside a few hours somewhere in your week to stop, to rest, to pray might be the first revision you could make.

It's important to remember that the ancients used a different calendar than our modern one. In fact, the very idea of a week is an arbitrary measure of time. A year, a day, even a month are based on cycles of the earth, the sun, and the moon. Some cultures in history have had ten-day or eight-day weeks, or no distinction of weeks, only years, months, and days.

Craig Harline's fascinating book *Sunday: A History of the First Day from Babylonia to the Super Bowl* explores this in great detail. He notes that the idea of a seven-day week came from Jewish, Babylonian, and Greek influences. The Greeks created a calendar with seven days, each named for what they called a planet, although those planets included the sun and moon. "They fixed the order of days in the week: Saturn Day was the first day, Sun Day the second, then Moon Day, Mars Day (Tuesday), Mercury Day (Wednesday), Jupiter Day (Thursday), and Venus Day (Friday).... So far, there was nothing that made Sun Day, the second day, or for that matter any other day, stand out; although the planets possessed different qualities and were honored with distinct rituals, all planetary days were basically equal in stature. The idea that one day in the week was superior to others came from another ancient seven-day system: that of the Jews."[14]

So while their pagan neighbors were developing a calendar based on the planets and their corresponding gods (Saturn Day was the day the god Saturn had most influence), the Jews had their own system of keeping track of time.

Harline adds, "Although the Jewish week wanted nothing to do with any planetary week, two seven-day systems born in the eastern Mediterranean could hardly avoid bumping into and influencing one another.... Jewish influence on the Roman week was apparent by the mid-first century, when a growing number of Roman pagans began observing a weekly rest day. Their initial choice seems to have been Saturn Day (Saturday), the first day of the planetary week, which fell on the same day as the Sabbath, seventh day of the Jewish week."[15]

In other words, the Jews' seventh day fell on the same day the Greeks and Romans had arbitrarily chosen as the first day of their week. "By at least A.D. 100 Romans too regarded Saturn Day no longer as the first day of their week but as the seventh. Naturally this caused every other planetary day to shift in Rome as well—including Sun Day, which became the new first day. Hence Jewish and Roman weeks were now aligned: The Jewish Sabbath and Roman Saturn Day were both the seventh day, and the Jewish first day was equal to the Roman first day, or Sun Day."[16]

As Christianity spread, Christians began calling the first day of the week the Lord's Day as a weekly commemoration of Christ's resurrection. But it also happened to be the day that many Roman pagans worshiped. Many early Christians rested on the traditional Jewish Sabbath but worshiped and celebrated the resurrection on the Lord's Day. Since it was, in their culture, an ordinary work day, the Christians often met to worship before or after work on the Lord's Day.

The Bible says that right after Jesus' resurrection, Jesus' followers "joined together constantly" (Acts 1:14) and that they spent time together, both in the temple and in their homes, every day. Daily. (See all of Acts 2, esp. vv. 46–47). One assumes the believers mostly had jobs or other obligations, although I'm guessing they didn't have hockey games or Little League or a sale at Home Depot to pull them away from getting together.

The book of Acts describes the growth of the church and the missionary journeys of the apostle Paul. Paul attended synagogue on Sabbath but apparently went there to argue: "Every Sabbath he reasoned in the synagogue, trying to persuade Jews and Greeks" (Acts 18:4). During the week, he worked as a tent maker, but on Sabbath, he engaged rigorously in trying to convince both Jews and Gentiles to follow Jesus.

Gradually, however, the church began gathering less frequently. Eventually, as the gospel spread, traditions evolved. Within a few decades, churches apparently had to be reminded to gather regularly, as evidenced in the book of Hebrews: "And let us consider how we may spur one another on toward love and good deeds, not giving up meeting together, as some are in the habit of doing, but encouraging one another—and all the more as you see the Day approaching" (10:24–25).[17]

Old Testament law says that the Sabbath is a day for rest and also "a day of sacred assembly" (Lev. 23:3). The early church, in some cases, seemed to be in the practice of meeting daily. In some churches today, members are expected to be at the church serving or attending services more than once a week. I do think that attending church should be part of our Sabbath practice, not as an obligation but to connect with the community we are a part of. If it is truly a day to love God and love others, then it makes sense to gather with others to worship God. Some people tell me they feel closer to God in nature than they do in church. I won't argue with that. I find that seeing God's handiwork in creation inspires me to worship as well. That's why a walk in the woods or even just around your neighborhood is a good Sunday-afternoon practice. But that doesn't give you a free pass to skip church, because part of why we attend church and serve within the body is so that we can be formed into the image of Christ. Our spiritual formation, as Robert Mulholland points out, is not for us alone but for the sake of others.[18] We offer others the gift of community. At least some of the others we are called to love are in our church. And we should choose a church based not just on what we get out of it but also on what we are able to put into it.

That being said, some ministers I interviewed said that they serve on Sunday but then take another day of the week (usually Saturday or Monday) for solitude, family time, and rest. Even if you are not an official minister, you may find that Sunday is a day when you are serving a lot, and you may need to set aside another day for Sabbath.

St. Ignatius, a first-century church father, writes that Christians should observe the Lord's Day as a festival and that the day before, Sabbath, should be spent in meditation on God's Word rather than focused on rituals of a meal and rest. In his letter to the Magnesians, Ignatius writes, "Let us therefore no longer keep the Sabbath after the Jewish manner, and rejoice in days of idleness." That letter instructed the early church to "keep the Sabbath after a spiritual manner, rejoicing in meditation on the law, not in relaxation of the body.... And after the observance of the Sabbath, let every friend of Christ keep the Lord's Day as a festival, the resurrection-day, the queen and chief of all the days [of the week]."[19]

Ignatius was concerned about "Judaizing," following Jewish practices, which he said was incompatible with living by grace.

In the first few centuries after Christ's death, many Christians followed this advice and observed both days—the Sabbath "after a spiritual manner" (or, sometimes, in a more Jewish manner, since that was their background) and the Lord's Day by attending church services, celebrating Christ's resurrection with the sacrament of communion.

Harline's book has fabulous detail on the history of Sunday observances through the centuries in various countries. (The French Sunday, for example, was much more lenient and pleasure-oriented than the English.) After the Reformation, Harline notes, "often hair-splitting arguments over Sunday did not stop with Catholics versus Protestants. For especially in the process of refuting Catholics, Protestants began to reveal angry disagreements among themselves."[20]

Harline offers plenty of insight on the Puritan Sabbath, citing Nicholas Bownd's 1595 work, *The Doctrine of the Sabbath*, a five-hundred-page tome outlining the proper observance of the Sabbath. "The 'cease from' element of the 'Sabbath' included ceasing not merely from work but from anything 'worldly,' which Bownd took to include play. Contrary to stereotypes, Puritans were not against all sport: rather, they opposed certain kinds of violent sport, such as bear-baiting and cockfighting, and all Sunday sport. Even lawful sport should cease on the Sabbath, argued Bownd. Sport's inherently playful character was not in keeping with the eternal matters that should prevail on that day."[21]

Sabbath rules over the years have not necessarily gone from strict to lenient. Rather, they've swung back and forth, from time to time, from place to place. The Puritans' strict interpretation was a reaction to the laxity they perceived in their culture. Just as religious leaders in Jesus' day had different interpretations of what it means to remember and observe the Sabbath, so have various Christian leaders through the ages. Martin Luther said the Sabbath was for the Jews, not for Christians, who considered every day holy. John Calvin, Harline notes, saw the Sabbath as a "perpetual institution" that God established for all people. "This did not mean that the specific rules and regulations of the Old Testament Sabbath still applied to Christians," Harline writes about Calvin's interpretation. "Instead it meant that the lasting spiritual truths behind the Sabbath commandment simply required a new form.... Calvin tried to exclude both the strict legalism and the excessive levity said to mark the Jewish Sabbath, and thus held up a 'moderate' Sabbath. He himself was said to have bowled on Sunday."[22]

My point with this little history lesson is simply to point out that traditions, and even calendars, evolve. They change; they are influenced by the culture around them. Some stricter Sabbatarians were inspired by what they perceived to be sinful behavior in the culture around them. When the Bible says "the seventh day," it might not necessarily mean the seventh day in our culture, because we are using a different calendar than existed in Old Testament times. The small appointment book I carry in my purse, for example, is set up showing Monday as the first day of the week, so that the weekend is actually at the week's end. In our culture, Sunday is, in some ways, the seventh day, since it is the second day of the weekend. For many of us, from a practical standpoint, the week begins Monday, when we head back to work after our busy weekends.

If you don't ever take a day, be it the seventh day, the first day, or any day, to focus on God and enjoy his rest, then getting hung up on which day becomes a stumbling block. The first step in a Sabbath Simplicity journey is to choose one day a week, to commit to practicing Sabbath on that day, and to be mindful about your practice rather than just letting things slide.

Since our culture generally still observes two days of rest (the typical workweek being, at least on paper, Monday through Friday), choose one of those days. I'd suggest the day you attend church services as the optimal day. If you are obligated to work on weekends (I'm talking employment, not household chores), choose one of the days you have off from work. If your church has a midweek service and you work on weekends, see if you can take that day off from work to make that your Sabbath. Or arrange to meet with your small group on whichever day you've chosen to practice Sabbath. Find a way to make community part of your Sabbath practice.

Keep it consistent. Don't choose a different day each week,

based on your convenience. Try it for at least six months. You may have to make adjustments, but give it time.

Once you get a little farther along in this journey, God may direct you to a specific day. Be attentive to his leading, but the important thing is simply to start this practice with whatever small steps you can.

living on grace

In practicing Sabbath, we rest because God rested. We imitate God and, in so doing, realize we are not God. But also we rest from accumulating, from striving after greater prosperity. In so doing, we cultivate contentment. We have time to remember that what we have is a gift from God. We live on grace on Sabbath, not by the working of our hands. And in community, we extend that grace to others. Sabbath is often the day we bring offerings to church. By doing so, we affirm that we have enough. And we begin to see that the poor, those who live on grace every day, should be of concern to us. We have enough — enough to be generous.

In resting, we are reminded that God provides for us. Even if we work hard, the ability to do so is a gift. Taking a day off affirms the generosity of God, because we notice that he provides enough (like the manna in the wilderness) for a day when we are not working or consuming. We reject the label "consumer" by refraining from commerce, both buying and selling. If we are out at the mall, are we trusting the provision of God? That we have enough? Not shopping is a way of saying, "I have enough stuff already."

And that truth ought to inform how we view our possessions and our work. All are gifts and are to be shared. Imitating God by keeping Sabbath seduces us into imitating him daily — to be gracious as God is gracious, to love as God loves, to care for those who hunger and thirst, both figuratively and literally.

rest for all

To observe Sabbath is to flatten social hierarchy. The Deuteronomy and Exodus commands have this in common: they both include a radically inclusive list of who is to be allowed to rest on Sabbath—everyone. Men and women, children, servants, aliens (strangers, that is, non-Jews), even animals. The Deuteronomy account goes so far as to list a few specific animals for good measure.

"Six days you shall labor and do all your work, but the seventh day is a Sabbath to the Lord your God. On it you shall not do any work, neither you, nor your son or daughter, nor your male or female servant, nor your ox, your donkey or any of your animals, nor any foreigner residing in your towns, so that your male and female servants may rest, as you do" (Deut. 5:13–14). It's as if God expected us to look for loopholes and wanted to make sure to close those off. It's not just men who get a day off but women too. It's not just free people but even slaves who should have a day to rest. And don't delegate your work to someone else, even your ox or your donkey.

This list sounds vaguely familiar, doesn't it? Compare it with this list: "There is neither Jew nor Gentile, neither slave nor free, neither male nor female, for you are all one in Christ Jesus" (Gal. 3:28). God does not discriminate on the basis of gender, race, or socio-economic status. All are invited; all are included. Jesus said, "Come to me, *all* you who are weary and burdened, and I will give you rest" (Matt. 11:28, emphasis mine). It's not rest for some but rest for all. It's not rest for those who are spiritually superior but rest for anyone who is weary and burdened. And Jesus is calling us not to come to work but to come to rest.

Sabbath symbolizes the spiritual rest we find only in intimacy with Jesus.

observe and remember

In the Hebrew tradition, Sabbath is not simply a day but a mind-set, a living and lived-in symbol. The day is the centerpiece of the week: anticipated for three days, practiced for one, and remembered for three days after.

Author Karen Mains points out that the two terms *observe* and *remember* are a part of living in Sabbath rhythm in the Jewish tradition. The three days prior to Sabbath, Jews would observe the Sabbath by preparing and anticipating. For the three days after, they would remember the beauty and rest of the day, and then the cycle would begin again. "Three days to look forward to Sabbath, then the high point, the day itself, then for observant Jews, because it was so special, they took three days to reflect back on its wonder."[23]

Sabbath is a central and important festival, a day to focus on God—by reading and studying the Scriptures, by enjoying the fruit of our labors, and also by loving others. We study, read, and discuss God's Word, not just for the sake of learning but so that our learning would inform our living the other six days. What we learn at church or in our personal devotions on Sabbath should fill us with truth that we take out to spill all over the world during the week.

We need to revise our view of economic reality and revise our priorities. Doing so will move us toward a richer experience of God and toward freedom. How can we revise our lives around Sabbath reality? That is what we will consider in the next chapter.

4

revising

A Shift from Rut to Rhythm

The rhythm of life for countless people ... emerges as one that oscillates between driven achievement (both on and off the job) and some form of mind-numbing private escape. This crazed rhythm, based on a distorted view of human reality, increasingly poisons our institutions, relationships and quality of life.
—**Tilden Edwards,** *Sabbath Time*

When my children were babies (they're not quite two years apart), Sundays felt exhaustingly similar to the rest of the week. I still changed diapers, wiped up endless spills, prepared meals, picked up toys that apparently scattered through the house of their own volition. But on Sunday morning, I had the added chore of getting my two babies up and dressed and out to church.

Because my husband is a realtor, he'd often head off to work on Sunday, just like any other day. Sometimes, he'd go to church with us but drive separately so he could leave to show a house right after the service. I drove by myself so much that I had a permit to park in our church's "One Parent" parking lot — premium parking right near the door to the children's classrooms, for single parents with two or more children under five. While I appreciated my church's effort to make life easier for adults outnumbered by the kids they were schlepping to church, I felt a bit sad every time I pulled into that lot.

During that draining season, I longed for a break but thought, "Moms don't get a day off." That stinks. And my husband didn't seem to get many days off, either. We were both self-employed, both stressed, both tired. We didn't seem to know how to rest. I read books that mentioned Sabbath. I thought about trying to practice it. I took some small steps, like not shopping on Sundays. But we had two preschoolers, and our jobs (I was freelance writing, parenting two preschoolers, and managing our home) made our schedule unpredictable.

In some seasons, you have to revise your expectations. In others, you actually have to revise your life. Part of what we do in Sabbath-keeping is to revise, to try a new direction or way of approaching things. That can help us get unstuck when we are overwhelmed and paralyzed.

Sabbath-keeping has caused me to revise my life, and sometimes my life has forced me to revise Sabbath. Sabbath-keeping has taught me and my family flexibility. It has changed both with the seasons of the year and with the seasons of our lives.

Over the years, I've tried various ways to figure out how to rest. Mandating it rarely worked. Inviting my family and others into a restful place was much more effective.

start where you are

Where does a Sabbath Simplicity journey begin? Right where you are.

When Jesus walked this planet, he invited people to follow him. He sought them out. Responding to his invitation requires us to revise our lives from the get-go. When we say yes to Jesus' offer of adoption and forgiveness and grace, we are never the same again. Our priorities shift because that grace comes when we choose to follow Jesus. But we start our journey wherever it is that Jesus finds us.

Luke's gospel tells of Jesus' invitation to Simon Peter, James, and John. They had a small fishing business, but Jesus said, "Let's revise: from now on you will catch people and invite them into my kingdom." Later he tells Matthew, "Follow me." The Bible says that all of them "left everything and followed him." (See Luke 5.)

In their culture, such an invitation signified great honor. Even so, these men (and other men and women who chose to follow Jesus) chose a radically different path than they'd previously followed. But that revision was only the beginning. Every time they turned around, Jesus would say something new or different. He spoke in riddles and parables, often confounding not only the crowds who followed him but his inner circle of friends as well. They'd scratch their heads or whisper to one another, wondering what he meant. Some even walked away.

But eventually they got it. They were changed; they revised their whole lives. How did Jesus do this? I believe his primary method for changing lives was, and is, spending time with people. Simply by being with people, Jesus transformed them.

Jesus walked around with his disciples, he stayed at their homes, he ate with them. When he traveled about teaching, they came along. They followed him. Jesus just hung out with them and looked for teachable moments. As a result, his followers (which included not only the twelve apostles but many other men and women) were radically changed. After Jesus died, Peter and John were preaching and healing, carrying on the ministry.

They were brought before the religious leaders for questioning. The religious leaders wanted to know where they got their power. The disciples answered fearlessly that they were healing in the name of Jesus.

"When they saw the courage of Peter and John and realized that they were unschooled, ordinary men, they were astonished and they took note that these men had been with Jesus" (Acts 4:13). My deep desire is that when other people look at my life and listen to my words, they will notice that apparently, I've been with Jesus. Time spent with him revises my life much more radically than any goal-setting or self-improvement plan.

Sabbath is a day when we can spend time with Jesus. It's so much more than just a day to chill. It's a day to rest in God's presence, to respond to Jesus' invitation, "Come to me, all you who are weary and burdened, and I will give you rest" (Matt. 11:28).

It sounds so simple. And yet to rest requires a bit of planning. We have to prepare. We have to say no, over and over. We've got to make some changes.

When we spend a day resting, focused only on loving God and loving others, we experience the presence of Jesus in simple things. We experience peace, the sacredness of the ordinary. What if we had a day focused not on entertainment but on true connectedness, a day when we unplug our electronics but plug in to others? Not to endlessly serve them but to know them. To engage with them and allow them to engage with us. To spend time, as Jesus did, and allow them to change us and us to change them.

Do you think taking an entire day off each week would be impossible? That may be true. You may have committed to far too many things, and you're stuck with those decisions. Or you may have been running at top speed for so long that your first gear simply doesn't work.

Thomas Merton writes, "To allow oneself to be carried away by a multitude of conflicting concerns, to surrender to too many demands, to commit oneself to too many projects, to want to help everyone in everything, is to succumb to violence."[1]

the only person you can change

Revising your life, getting unstuck (whether from inertia or overdrive), is a process. Often we realize subconsciously that it won't be easy, so we come up with excuses for why we simply cannot change things. Usually we try to blame it on other people.

In my work I have the opportunity to speak to and hear from women from all around the country. In conversations with them about Sabbath, I often hear things like "my husband is not on board" or "my husband doesn't act like a spiritual leader." (Some can't say what that should look like exactly; others have highly detailed dreams about what they would like their husband to do.) Variations include "my family doesn't want to do this," "it would be a lot of work," or simply, "I could never do that."

Our tendency is to want to revise other people or their actions, but really, the only person we can truly change is ourselves.

So here is what works for me: I try to rest in a way that is inviting to my family. I don't make the kids stay home, but I won't take them shopping. Often, the kids have friends over to hang out. I *model* quietness. I am available to listen but not to wait on them hand and foot. Until recently, Scot's been mostly unaware that I was being intentional about my Sabbath practice, because I didn't really talk about it much. At this point, we don't have a lot of rituals. The day is marked by things we don't do — shopping, housework, or laundry. We don't hurry.

But the thing is, because I didn't want to push him, I didn't communicate what I was doing. I hoped he'd notice. Instead, he'd come home from working on a Sunday and start telling the kids to do their chores. It put me in a difficult place.

So we are totally in process on this. The revisions continue as I try to figure out how to invite my husband into this practice, which has felt like too overwhelming a task for most of our marriage. I'm realizing that I need to frame things for my family a little bit, to point out and name the things we are doing sometimes. When I have talked to him about it, asked him about what he'd like to include, he's had some great ideas—reading the Bible or other books with the kids, taking a bike ride together, and so on. He likes to have people over, since he's more of an extrovert. I said that would be fine but I'd like to have him help with the practical aspects of that hospitality.

My daughter, who gets her extroversion from her daddy, also suggests inviting other families over for Sunday supper. I, in turn, invite her to help me prepare for such visits. Which she is glad to do.

Invite your family to practice Sabbath with you, but give them the freedom to take the journey at their own pace. Before telling your husband, "I want you to be the leader. Let's go! Step up!" which might feel a lot like pressure, consider this option: what would happen if you said to your spouse, "I'd really like Sundays to be a Sabbath, a day that's peaceful and restful. I'd like to focus on loving God and loving others, and to teach our kids to do that too. So what I'm going to do is make sure the house is cleaned up, that our schedule is cleared, that we have meals or at least some leftovers prepared ahead of time. I'm going to do my best to make our home a haven, especially on Sundays. How does that sound to you?"

Most guys I know would think that's great. Then say, "I'd love to do this together. What are some things you think our family would enjoy doing together on Sunday? What do you think would make it fun, yet restful?"

Then whatever he suggests, whether taking a bike ride together, playing outside with the kids, or discussing a portion of Scripture, say, "Great. Could you run point on that aspect of the day?"

If he's not interested in participating, then that is his choice. That shouldn't keep you from, say, at a meal, asking your family questions to get them talking about what they learned at church that day or inviting them to converse. And it should not keep you from resting on Sabbath. You can't control other people, but you also don't have to let them control you. For some of us, just living that last sentence will take some major revisions of attitude and action. If your husband is particularly resistant to Sabbath-keeping, you may want to start with just one simple practice. In the Jewish Sabbath tradition, rabbis would often encourage married couples to make love on the Sabbath—a true act of recreation, I suppose. Admittedly, it is not part of the law's requirements, but it is definitely within the law's allowance. One of my readers, a working mom with three young children, says she and her husband have made this a part of their Sabbath, with great benefit to their marriage.

"Several months ago, I was leafing through a magazine and came upon a 'spice up your marriage' type article," she says. "I was intrigued to read that in the Jewish tradition, Sabbath-keeping includes lovemaking on Friday nights. No matter what happens, be it busyness, weariness, or even conflict, this 'Sabbath-keeping' activity is a Friday night tradition. As you can imagine, my husband was game to institute this as part of our weekend routine. I really believe that if you aren't intentional about reconnecting, be it physically or otherwise, you will experience a slow but deadly drift in your marriage. So this unspoken part of the Sabbath really gets us back together as one, so that we can begin the weekend reunited in body and spirit. Although it's not always an easy tradition to keep, it has made such a difference in the way that we approach the weekend together; both of us are more willing and able to honor the other's needs and make sacrifices for each other and for our family as a whole."

A key part of revising your life is simply being intentional. In certain seasons of marriage, it's easy to get too busy to find time to talk to each other, let alone enjoy sex. But if your husband is a bit hesitant about Sabbath, this might be just the ticket for getting him on board. Joking aside, knowing that you will make time to be together can add a bit of a spark to your relationship, give you something to look forward to. It can also be an incentive to work out conflicts quickly.

Talk about your desire for a day of rest with the people you live with. But remember that any change will require some discussion and perhaps negotiation. Sara, a reader, says she and her husband are still working out what Sabbath means. "Having a Sabbath takes a lot of negotiating between me and my husband," Sara says. "We each want time for ourselves, which requires the other one to watch the kids, but we want to have time as a family as well. It is often hard to squeeze all of this into one day, but we are learning to take turns and give each other a rest from whatever our 'work' is (his job for him, and kids and housework for me). I have also begun to see that giving my children my undivided attention is a good activity for Sabbath; it is something I don't do enough of the rest of the week. My husband is a pastor and has Mondays off, so my five-year-old knows that Monday is Daddy's day off and always gets excited because he enjoys his time with his daddy so much. This has made me realize the value of kids having a routine they can count on, like one day a week that is for having fun and spending time with Daddy. I am beginning to realize that I need that routine as well. As a mom of little ones, my work is never done, and Sabbath in a way gives me permission to rest even though the work isn't done. It is something I look forward to and gets me through the work of the rest of the week. This was not something I grew up with; the mentality always was 'finish your work first, and then you can rest or play,' so it has been a shift of mindset for me."

I think for most of us, that's a good place to begin—to change our thinking about what to include in our Sabbath practice.

revise with grace

When we think about revising, we often get caught up in an "all or nothing" mentality, which is counterproductive, to say the least. As you move toward Sabbath Simplicity, figure out which steps you can take. Take one at a time, rather than feeling you have to revamp your life and the lives of the people you live with all at once. Revise with grace. Even if you are in a different place in your spiritual journey than your spouse, you can still walk in the same direction. Rather than focusing on what you perceive to be your husband's shortcomings or your differences, put your energy into setting up the day so that you can rest, so that you are available relationally. Gently invite others to join you.

I was praying about writing this chapter today, and I thought, "My Sabbath is too simple." And God and I had a good laugh over that one. It really just doesn't need to be that complicated. After all, Jesus said, the Sabbath is for people.

One woman I met complained that the neighbor kids knocked on the door while they were trying to have family time. I wonder what would happen if you invited the neighbor kids in but held firmly to an agenda of reading some Scripture together and asking each person in the room to share the highlight of their week? How might you speak to those kids of

God's love (without ever saying it out loud) simply by sitting down and playing a board game with your children and including them in that? Or inviting them to join you for a meal, not in front of the television but around a table, during which you have conversation and talk about where you have seen God in your lives that week?

That being said, I do think it is important to set boundaries around certain times so that you can do things with just your immediate family. That means you'll have to say no to others and ask your family to join you in spending time together. Ask for their input on what you'll do with that time. If your neighbors are particularly invasive, you may have to take your family on an outing in order to get time alone. Many people I spoke to said taking a walk, either alone or with family or friends, is a Sabbath practice that is restful yet invigorating.

Whose attitude can you revise, really? Only your own. But changing yourself will change every relationship you're part of. If you change *your* steps, the whole dance starts to change.

Your goal in revising is not to whip others into shape but to allow Christ to transform your soul. What do you need to do to rest? Often the resistance of others is born of the fear that they'll have more things they have to do or simply of a resistance to change.

Rather than telling the people you live with, "Here's what you have to do," simply change what you are doing. You may want to tell your family, "Here's what I'm going to do," so that they are aware of what you are doing. But they have to choose whether to join you.

Have you ever been really frazzled and then come into the presence of someone who is calm, collected? A person who doesn't let your anxiety infect them but, rather, calms you simply by speaking quietly and refusing to become flustered? What if you could be that person in your home? What if you chose to rest and to enjoy being quiet? What if you said, "Today, I will be a listener; if people want to talk, I'm here"? Allow yourself to be interruptible, at least for conversation, but not for running errands.

Creating a restful atmosphere requires preparation. So in the days prior to Sabbath, do the chores you will not do that day: clean the house, do the laundry, shop for groceries. You may have to revise your schedule to do this, but it will create a restful atmosphere.

It takes planning. But it's not impossible. When you have a guest come to your house, you work ahead of time (such as cleaning and shopping) so that you can spend time with them. On Sabbath, Jesus is your honored guest.

Rather than trying to force your family to stay home, make home an inviting place on Sabbath. Remember that you cannot give away what you don't have. To keep Sabbath means to stop. So just stop. Stop working, stop telling people what to do, stop running your household. See if you can model restfulness well enough that your calm pervades your home and even your family. This may take repeated attempts, but even if no one else changes, you will be transformed by the experience. It won't happen all at once, but that's okay. Take it one step at a time.

Pray and decide which day you will observe Sabbath. Don't switch it from week to week, but choose. Then arrange your life around keeping that practice.

How much Sabbath is enough? Do you really need to do a full twenty-four hours? Wouldn't God be satisfied with just a few hours on Sunday afternoon? For some of us, that's all we can manage, and it's a good start. But God invites us to rest for a day, and that's the goal. But if you don't rest at all, ever, then as a first step, you may want to decide to do half a Sabbath. Decide that by sunset Saturday, whether or not your tasks are done, you will simply stop. You will have to prepare on Friday as well, making sure the pantry and fridge are stocked, the house is picked up, and so on. Saturday afternoon, finish straightening up your home, prepare a meal to share with friends or family, and as the sun sets, enjoy it.

If you have small children, get them into their jammies before dinner—or better yet, let your husband handle that task while you prep a simple meal.

Spend the evening in conversation or enjoying a good book. Take a few moments to read a section of Scripture and talk about it with the people you live with, if they are open to it. If they are not, then read it yourself. Take a walk if it's pleasant out, or sit by the fire and drink hot cocoa if it's cold. Play a board game with your family or read a story together. If your church has services on Saturday evening, you may want to attend them.

Go to bed knowing that God is watching over you. Wake up in the morning and spend a few moments in prayer, just listening, just enjoying God's presence.

That's half a Sabbath right there. Could you manage that? I bet you could. If you attend church on Sunday, go to services. You've made it through almost three-quarters of a twenty-four-hour period of rest. But this last gap—between the last amen at church service and sunset—that's where our obedience is tested. This time, perhaps five or six hours, has the potential to undo all the benefits of our Sabbath's first half. This is where Sabbath-keeping becomes a spiritual discipline, especially when it's new to us. That's why we should start as simply as possible.

What things do you want to be free of? What are the "have-tos" of your life? What do you *have* on Sunday?

Part of what you have on Sundays is connected to what you have said yes to during the rest of the week. If you have children and they are involved in several sports or other activities, your Sundays may end up kind of crazy. You may have to revise your schedule. Early on, we decided that our children could participate in one sport at a time. One. They were also allowed, if they wanted, to do one artistic pursuit, such as music or art. So they had at most two activities. And piano lessons or art classes didn't fall on Sundays, as sports games tend to do. If you have children and you revise their schedules in this way, you'll find that your Sundays will change.

All of us have certain obligations that must be fulfilled. But can we be honest? Sometimes we women take care of everything, whether or not it's our job. We complain, "Why do I have to do everything around here?" I'll tell you why—because we won't let anyone else do it, because they don't do it right. Or we never ask for help. For many moms, just letting Daddy bathe the children, make dinner (even if it is soup and sandwiches), or do the dishes would give us the break we want. Often when others try to help us, we discourage them by being critical or redoing what they've done (pointing out their incompetence without saying a word). Faced with that, would you want to continue to try to help, or just give up?

The Bible says we should humble ourselves, that we should not consider ourselves better than others. If we think we are the only ones who can do things correctly, we are giving in to the sin of pride.

Let things be done to different standards; allow for imperfection for one day. Really, this is not about letting things slide. It's about exercising humility and building trust. And trust is indeed a huge part of Sabbath. In keeping Sabbath, we trust that God's love is not something to be earned but a gift to be received. We trust that God will provide even when we stop earning, working, acquiring.

learning to trust

Trust, for most of us, requires a major life revision. We say we trust God, but do we live that way? Our experience, perhaps, has made us wary of trusting others. Our workaholic tendencies are often driven by fear—that we will not have enough; that if we don't accomplish, we don't have value. Sabbath-keeping challenges us to experience the provision of God and the un-earned love of God. It's one thing to say, "God loves me no mat-ter what," but to have a day when we accomplish nothing and feel God's pleasure—that's a transformational experience.

Cec Murphy says his Sabbath journey has been about trust and knowing that God loves him apart from his accomplish-ments. Such a truth is sometimes elusive for those who've ac-complished a lot. Cec and his wife, Shirley, are empty nesters living in the Atlanta area. Cec is a prolific writer, having writ-ten or cowritten 104 books and more than seven hundred ar-ticles. He makes his living primarily as a ghostwriter, taking other people's ideas and shaping them into books. He's taught at over two hundred writers' conferences. At seventy-three, he still works full-time and has no plans to retire.

For most of his life, Cec says, he was a bit of a workaholic, even in seemingly spiritual careers as a missionary, a pastor, a teacher, and an author. Today, he's still driven and highly dis-ciplined. But he's found that he's a much happier man, and no less productive than before, now that he has incorporated the practice of Sabbath rest into his life.

He grew up in what he describes as "a very chaotic home." His father was an alcoholic but never missed a day of work. Although his dad retired, he kept working his three-acre farm until he died at age eighty-four. His mother took him to church occasionally, but Cec found it boring and stopped his sporadic attendance when he was eleven. "At age sixteen, I learned the word agnostic, and that seemed to describe me, so I called my-self one," he says.

In his early twenties, he began asking big questions about the meaning of life. One day, walking past a used bookstore, he noticed a copy of *Magnificent Obsession* by Lloyd C. Douglas. The title intrigued him, and he read the book. "It's about a man who gives himself to others because his life is transformed by words from the Sermon on the Mount. Douglas never gives the reference," Cec says, "so I decided to read the New Testament to find that verse. I read all the way to the middle of Romans without finding the verse. One day I put down my New Testament and said, 'I believe this.'"

He started going to church, where he eventually met his wife, whom he describes as a "cradle Christian" who had grown up in a strong faith. She never told him he ought to slow down or that he needed to practice Sabbath, but she modeled it. "She's always taken time for herself, but she didn't try to tell me how to live my life. She's usually figured these things out way ahead of me," he says.

Many people half his age aren't nearly as productive and busy as Cec is. "I have an enormous amount of energy," he says. When his children were young, he and his family served as missionaries in Kenya for six years. "When you are a missionary or a pastor, Sunday is your biggest work day, or at least the most visible work day. At that stage of my life, I was more afraid of being lazy than anything else. Sabbath never occurred to me."

Returning from Kenya, he went back to school to work on his master's while working part-time as a pastor. "I think in those days I saw sleep as something to overcome," he says. He would get by on five or six hours of sleep a night and never took a day off. He says most men "brag about how little sleep they get."

For fourteen years, he worked as a pastor and also wrote books, and during that time, a couple in his church expressed concern that he never took time off. They encouraged him to take Fridays off.

"The trouble with a seven-day week is that you get results," he admits. "The harder I worked, the more praise I got. But then I started noticing in the Bible how much the Old Testament talks about Sabbath. And I thought, 'I never relax; I never take a long vacation.'"

His intense pace and extraordinary productivity earned him praise from some people, but looking back, he says, "I did a disservice to my kids. I remember one day I was with my son — he was a teenager — and he told me that he didn't want to be a preacher when he grew up. When I asked him why, he said, 'Because you never have enough time for your kids.' Wow, that hit me."

Still, the idea of taking a day off scared him, especially after he left the pastorate and began writing full-time. Being self-employed frightened him a bit. He was afraid they'd "end up living under a bridge or something" if he didn't make enough from writing to support his family.

But he kept reading the Old Testament passages on Sabbath, and also some passages in the New Testament that reminded him that the body is the temple of the Holy Spirit. He began to think about how not resting affected him. "I realized I was mistreating God's temple," he says.

He also remembers reading about a study done during World War II in England. Workers were put on a schedule of working twenty-one days in a row, then having several days off, and their productivity was measured. By way of comparison, the workers were also put on a six-days-on, one-day-off schedule. On each schedule, the number of days worked was the same. Yet when they got to take one day off per week, their productivity doubled.

Still, take a whole day off? To do nothing? Cec could not even conceive of such a thing. So he started slowly, just taking one or two hours after church simply to do nothing, to relax. "After a while, I gradually made it three hours, then four," he laughs.

At about that time, he did some ghostwriting for some people in the Seventh-day Adventist Church. "They showed me that it is okay to let go and just enjoy the day," he said. "The secret of the Sabbath is to enjoy not doing something. If you have to do certain things, you find ways to cheat."

That was ten years ago. Now, he stops working at about noon on Saturday. That afternoon or evening, he may check email, but unless he's under a tight deadline, he won't write. That evening, he'll put the finishing touches on his Sunday-school lesson for the week, sometimes comparing notes on the lesson with Shirley.

Sundays, the Murphys go to church, where Cec teaches an adult Sunday-school class. Sometimes he and Shirley will go out to lunch with friends from church. But he does no writing on Sundays (except when an editor demanded rewrites on a manuscript with a three-day turnaround). He says, "Sometimes I play in the yard," where he's learned to enjoy gardening. "I discovered that I have a green thumb, but it's really play, not work. The amazing thing is, you're really fresher on Monday when you come back to work."

Sabbath is not just a day, Cec has learned. "Some people think that you go full speed for six days and then just stop, but that's not right," he says. "The other six days need a rhythm."

A disciplined and structured person by nature, and a long-time runner, Cec runs about thirty miles a week. His day starts with a run at 5:00 a.m., and five days a week, he's at the computer writing by 7:30 or 8:00 a.m., where he works until lunch. After an hour break, he's back on the computer until 4:00 or 5:00 p.m. But then, he stops. That's an essential part of the rhythm of his life as well. To engage fully, but then to disengage from his work. And to engage in quiet connection with his wife.

"I've learned to enjoy my evenings," he says. "Shirley and I are avid readers, so sometimes in the evening we'll just be sitting on either side of the room, reading different books."

Still, Cec and Shirley are not legalistic. "If you lay it down as law, you're sunk," he said. "The Sabbath principle is that you rest so you can enjoy your life, enjoy the fruit of your labor."

While some people do that by retiring, Cec has no interest in that. His career is going quite well. His book *Ninety Minutes in Heaven*, which he wrote at age seventy-two with Don Piper, topped the bestseller lists and was made into a movie.

"I have no plans to retire, but I've started resting more between projects," he said. "When I finish a draft of a book, I give myself a half day off. And two years ago, after I finished a major project, I took from January to March off. I am trying to find ways to enjoy my life."

That's not easy when the culture outside us, and a certain drive within us, pushes us to accomplish, and even identifies us by our achievements.

Cec observes, "Most men—and increasingly in our culture, women—identify themselves with their job. When people meet me, the first thing they ask is, 'What do you do?' In our culture, productivity is our way to express value. I don't know anyone who ever expresses that they don't have enough to do."

stage of life

Cec and Shirley will do Sabbath differently than a family with young children. Their life as empty nesters looks nothing like mine—they don't have to attend soccer games or provide care or supervision to their children.

Life has seasons. Sabbath-keeping is a spiritual practice that has some flexibility. The outward practice must be shaped by the inward reality of your relationship with God, but it's also shaped by your circumstances.

What season of life are you in? Are you focused on career? Young children? Ministry? Caring for aging parents? Getting close to retirement? Adapt your practice to your season of life, because what you can do (and choose not to do) on Sabbath depends a lot on the stage of life you are in. If you have children in diapers, the work of changing diapers and feeding the kids continues 24/7. You cannot let those basic things slide for a day.

But you can revise the space between those obligations. And you can, for one day, choose to approach those things more mindfully, more slowly. Think of your care for your children as a way of loving Jesus, as if it were him you are feeding, bathing, dressing, even changing. Jesus said, "For I was hungry and you gave me something to eat, I was thirsty and you gave me something to drink.... I needed clothes and you clothed me" (Matt. 25:35 – 36). Meditate on that verse as you care for your children, as you feed them lunch or help them get dressed.

Victoria, a mother of six I chatted with via email, says her Sabbath practice includes long afternoon naps for everyone, including the children. The older children sometimes play quietly in their room during nap time, but the day is one of rest.

A mom of two young children told me she would love to practice Sabbath but simply cannot because her children are just two and four, too young. I told her she could easily practice Sabbath if she was willing to adjust expectations and adapt Sabbath-keeping to her season of life — to let go of the "ought to" list in her head that says how Sabbath should be practiced and to start the journey with small steps.

For example, if she were to make a practice of going to bed early on Saturday night, that would be a step toward making Sabbath restful. If she got a good night's rest on Saturday night, got up, and went to church with her family, that would be nearly half a Sabbath spent in rest and worship. And that would be a good starting point. Because getting a two-year-old and a four-year-old out the door for church might even feel like work, part of her Sabbath practice might be to ask her husband to partner with her in getting the children up, fed, and dressed. She wouldn't have to do a whole day of prayer and Bible study or sitting doing nothing.

From there, she could slowly, over time, stop doing things she doesn't like to do (like laundry or running errands) and start doing things she likes to do (like cuddling with her kids or reading the Sunday paper). She could add to the practice of sleeping and attending church a few simple rituals—adding them one at a time, slowly, as she explores the practice. For example, she could ask her husband to give her a half hour to go for a walk alone or sit in a comfy chair and read. She could nap when her children napped. She could teach her children to put their plates in the dishwasher so she wouldn't have to do dishes. (And yes, a four-year-old can learn to rinse and put his plastic plate and cup in the dishwasher! The two-year-old might need some help but should be invited to do some small part of it.)

I hope I planted a seed in her mind, but she seemed to think that since it wasn't an entire day of rest, it wouldn't count somehow. I wish I could have introduced her to Nicole, whom I met at another retreat. She and her husband have found a way to practice Sabbath with three preschoolers in their home.

the three r's

I met Nicole when I led a retreat for her church in Richmond, Virginia. Nicole is a volunteer director of women's ministries and led the team that organized the retreat. She has three kids under the age of five and also has a counseling practice, where she works part-time, mostly counseling teenage girls.

She and her husband have found that in this busy season of

life, they've had to revise what Sabbath-keeping is and create life-giving traditions.

"I've often thought that my family doesn't keep the Sabbath as it should. (Don't you hate those shoulds?) It felt like a huge area of my life that I would get to ... later," she says. "When the kids are older, when I can breathe, when I finish just trying to get the dishes done. But then I realized that we do keep a Sabbath in my home. Here are the three things that we keep each weekend:

"My husband recognizes that mothering is a huge responsibility and sometimes a strain for me. We agree that the relentless pace of parenting can drain both of us. I remember Dave saying once, 'I really love these kids. It's just that they are always ... here.'

"Because I'm home with them during the week, Dave honors that on the weekends by helping me get my three R's ... reading, running, and resting. (Yes, we actually talk about the three R's and call them such!) The reading meets my need to engage intellectually and feed my brain. Running keeps me strong physically, recharged mentally, and refilled spiritually, as it is one of my best prayer times. The resting provides the opportunity for complete stillness and solitude, as well as a chance to prepare for the week ahead. These recharging activities naturally renew my stamina for the kids, which frees Dave up with the opportunity to putter in the yard, watch some sports, or nap on the couch (hopefully, while watching sports, which is truly a holy experience for him). I love seeing the kids cuddle up with him on the couch and learn the art of just 'being.'"

So Nicole and Dave, instead of giving up or saying Sabbath ought to look a certain way, are finding what revives and rejuvenates them. They've also spread things out over the weekend. They usually try to spend a few hours Saturday doing something as a family—anything from going to a museum to playing in the yard.

"Although the children don't recognize the intentionality behind it, Dave and I feel that we are creating space for them to observe the Sabbath along with us," Nicole says. "To be honest, sometimes it is easier to go our separate ways ... divide and conquer with the kids rather than stay together. But we make the choice to do the together things, even if it isn't as convenient or effective for us. It keeps us sharpening one another and parenting side-by-side, rather than one at a time."

If you are married with kids, do you have some time during your weekend to "parent side-by-side"? Or are you each driving children in different directions?

letting go of legalism

The religious leaders of Jesus' day criticized him for many things, but it seems that most often he caught flak for what he did or didn't do on the Sabbath.

I write a column for a Christian website. When I posted a column about Sabbath, I got a lot of questions from readers, mostly about which day of the week it should be and what activities are allowed or are not allowed. My readers, though they would not have said so, were asking me about the rules. They seemed almost to crave legalism. Many were eager to engage me in debate or to take me to task for how I had broken what they considered to be the rules. Ambiguity is uncomfortable for most of us. But Jesus' main rule was to love God and love others. There's a lot of leeway (or what some might call ambiguity) in that. But there's also a lot of freedom. As I wrote earlier, part of what we are called to as followers of Jesus is to work out, in the context of community, what it means to follow Jesus' teaching.

As you begin talking about Sabbath and shaping your Sabbath practice, do you find yourself tempted to be legalistic? Does your church community support you? Connecting to community is an important part of Sabbath practice. Is your church community lax about Sabbath-keeping? Or overly strict?

While it's a hard question to ask, we need to at least consider it: does my church support my efforts to practice Sabbath? If not, do I need to prayerfully seek another church? Or is God calling me to be an agent of revision in my church home? That's something to think about and to pray for God's direction in.

While it's easy to look at the prohibitive perspective of Sabbath (what we say no to), I think we are much more likely to embrace a practice that invites us to exercise freedom and invites us to say yes. When we let go of legalism, we can say yes to joy, yes to connecting with the people we love. We can revise our schedules so that Sabbath is a day when we are free — free from doing housework, free from being a consumer, free from the stress of watching television news, which only assists us in finding a crisis, somewhere in the world, anytime day or night.

For teachers, ministers, and committed church volunteers, Sunday may not feel like a day of freedom. Even if you love your ministry, it can sometimes drain you. If we have to serve on Sunday, we may need another day to rest.

Because Marsha, a thirty-one-year-old mom and a Lutheran minister, is a ministry leader who "works" serving others on Sunday, she and her family decided to celebrate Sabbath together on Saturdays. In this, she found freedom to connect with family and friends, and she found renewed energy for her ministry. She wrote to me about her family's Sabbath practice, which she tells me was inspired in part by my book *Breathe*.

"Your chapter on Sabbath-keeping changed our family's spiritual life," she says. "My daughter, who was three at the time, now had one day out of seven that she knew she could look forward to having a 'God and family day,' as she called it. Now, two years later, Saturday is undoubtedly her favorite day of the week because she knows we will be disciplined not to clean or run errands but instead will spend time with family and friends and each other. That day is filled with time in the outdoors, always making that time holy. We often marvel at God's handiwork in creation as we set apart this one day of the week to enjoy these beautiful things which God has given to us."

What has made Sabbath-keeping possible for Marsha and her family is their determination simply to keep it and to let God guide them. Don't expect perfection, but be consistent.

Marsha is intentional about not running errands or doing housework. She sets herself free from that. But she also abstains from things that we sometimes think are helpful but often end up monopolizing our time. This abstinence is not legalistic but life-giving. And she added it only after she'd been on her Sabbath Simplicity journey for quite a while.

"We take a media Sabbath. No computer, no cell phone, no movies, no TV. This second component of our Sabbath came after we made it through the first year feeling so much closer to God and to one another," she says.

Because her daughter is young, Marsha and her husband use the day as an opportunity to teach her the why behind what now feels normal to her. "We speak very intentionally to our child about why we do this. This is not merely a day off of work and cleaning. This is our day to slow down and let God talk to us and for us to listen in return."

I think naming for your children what you are doing, so that they notice and remember it, is a huge step.

"Sabbath-keeping has also deeply affected my ministry," Marsha adds. "I just received my first call as a Lutheran minister with a focus on faith formation, and Sabbath-keeping is almost always introduced when I talk about ways to be centered on

God. I can teach it and preach it because I have lived it for two years and can share the exciting way in which it has changed our entire family's faith, strengthened our relationship with God, and transformed me into a much different minister—one who strives to walk the walk, not just teach it; one who strives to give God the space God deserves; one who strives to keep God as the center of everything else going on in her life, because the notion of being 'balanced' in this complex world is almost an impossible task. This is not to say that I have in any way perfected it, but there is certainly an intentionality in my life, our family's life, to return to God as home base. In an ever-increasingly demanding world filled with complex relationships, technology, and dynamics, resulting in an overwhelming need to compartmentalize our lives, the strength and vitality provided by Sabbath-keeping allow us to respond with God at our core, which is exactly where God deserves to be."

Marsha and her family have found freedom in Sabbath-keeping, in having a "God and family day" that is not legalistic but life-giving.

creating rituals

While we don't want to get caught up in legalism, I believe part of what we long for in our whirlwind culture is rituals—regular practices that serve as anchors in time, that hold us steady when things seem confused.

Rituals may seem like things we "have to" do, but they are simply ways of arranging and organizing our lives. They're regular practices. I recently realized that the word ritual is embedded in the word spiritual: spi*ritual*. A ritual can be something we do to get our minds and bodies to shift gears or to mark events or occasions. They often help us to be mindful in our spiritual practices.

Some people go into the same room or sit in the same chair each morning to pray. That ritual creates a sort of sacred space, and their bodies and souls relax when they even enter that space.

For example, many women I know find the ritual of a hot bath before bedtime relaxing and restorative. A cup of coffee and a few moments of reflective silence are a morning ritual for me, a routine that wakes up my brain, then my soul.

One ritual we have in our family, unrelated to Sabbath, is that on each person's birthday, we go around the dinner table and each person has to say a few things about the birthday person — what they like or admire about them, what they've noticed are the talents or strengths of that person. It's a ritual the kids won't let us skip, even on the grown-ups' birthdays. It brings life and joy to our family.

When my parents visit, we go out for pancakes on Saturday morning. When they are not here, my kids don't care about going to IHOP. But if we try to skip this part of my parents' visit, we get loud complaints. It's a ritual.

Ask God to give you some rituals that will make Sabbath meaningful. One ritual God recently gave to me is this: as the sun sets on Saturday evening, I turn off the computer. As it shuts down, I say a simple prayer of thanks for the work I've accomplished during the week, with God's help. I thank him for the gift of being able to work in a field I love. And when I turn on the computer again, either after sunset on Sunday or early Monday morning, I say another little prayer, thanking him for Sabbath rest and dedicating the writing, the emails, the research that will be done on the computer in the coming week to his glory.

Sabbath rituals don't mean that every Sabbath is the same, but they are ways of setting the day apart, of being intentional. Some rituals will be weekly, others less frequent.

One ritual that I engage in (not every week, but often) is to play music that is restful—usually it's classical music—on Sunday. In the winter, I will often put on Mozart and light a fire in the fireplace. These sounds and smells are a subtle signal to my family that I am in rest mode. They create a cozy atmosphere in our home that invites others to rest as well.

Summer Sundays often include a ritual of gardening. While some see gardening as work, I try to make Sundays in the garden a day when I don't do heavy lifting. Mostly I am puttering.

Some families I know like to stop at the bakery for donuts after church, a ritual the kids enjoy. In fact, many rituals can be created around food.

share a meal

Some of you perhaps grew up with the tradition of sharing a large family meal on Sundays. The downside of that large meal is that often, the women in the family are working hard to prepare it and then to clean up.

So how can you have a day of rest but still create food rituals?

Remember that we are on a journey of Sabbath Simplicity. And even rituals can have flexibility. Create a ritual of cooking a double meal (twice as much as your family normally consumes) on Friday. Then enjoy the leftovers on Sunday.

One informal ritual that sometimes fell on Sunday nights when the kids were small was to invite our close friends the Fischers over. We'd order Chinese food, the kids would play together, and the adults would play euchre. Since they've got five kids, it was fun, noisy, and felt like a big family gathering, but we didn't have to cook. They tended to have busy weekends, but Sunday night was a time we could just relax together.

I'm a big proponent of family meals. Even when I was single,

I purposely lived with a group of other single women. I worked an afternoon shift, so I wasn't home for dinner during the week. My housemates worked long hours and would tend to grab something on the way home. But on the weekends, we would gather as a family. We'd cook and enjoy a meal together. Time shared builds community. Food shared takes those bonds even deeper.

If your life is hectic and out of control to the point where you don't gather at least once a week with people you care about to break bread together, that is a great place to start revising your life. Remember that Sabbath Simplicity is not just how you live on Sundays but also how you live throughout your week.

For example, do you have a plan for gathering with your family during the week — whether for meals or just time together? Does your schedule allow it? In our family, the older the kids get, the more challenging this has become. Scot's job sometimes keeps him out in the evenings. His real-estate clients usually want to look at homes after they finish work, which means the dinner hour. My daughter plays on a soccer team that has evening practices, which adds another challenge. But we manage to gather for an evening meal several times each week. How? By doing some advance decision-making. This is key to all Sabbath practice.

Advance decision-making is simply deciding ahead of time, rather than in the moment, that you will do something and arranging your life around that decision. For example, if you want to increase your fitness level, you could try exercising whenever you feel like it. That might work, if you happen to like to exercise. (Don't laugh, some people do!) But if you are like most people, your tendency would be to let it slide. If you really want to become more fit, you have to do more than just hope you'll do it. You must decide ahead of time that you'll get up and run every morning or go to the gym Monday, Wednesday, and Friday after work. Then when it's time to go, you don't ask yourself, "Well, do I feel like going?" You just go, because you've decided ahead of time to do it.

So when it comes to family meals, I put them on the calendar. I plan the menu for the week so I'm not staring helplessly into the pantry at 5:00 p.m. If you think you don't have time to plan, that's a sure sign that you are too busy. I look at the calendar and figure out when the kids will be home. And at that time (which sometimes varies) we set the table and sit down, even if we are only having sandwiches and soup or scrambled eggs. Meals are more than an opportunity to refuel our bodies. They are a chance to reconnect spiritually, emotionally, and physically, to look into each other's eyes and affirm what we say we know—that we love one another.

During the week, we aim for a set time that accommodates carpool schedules, although as I've mentioned, we don't have activities every night. By saying no to overscheduling, we're free to say yes to family time. About half the time, Scot is working, although he can sometimes sneak home between working at the office and meeting a client to sit down with us for a few moments. Or he'll ask if we can have dinner at a certain time to accommodate his ever-shifting schedule, and if he gives me enough notice, I'll try to accommodate him. Planning must be tempered with flexibility: sometimes you have to call an audible instead of going with the playbook. But if Scot can't be at the table right away, that doesn't prevent the rest of us from gathering to eat, talk, and connect. We communicate clearly about our schedule, but if he's not able to join us, or if he's late, we don't wait for him. We simply gather with the three of us. And I make sure to ask the kids, "What was the highlight of your day?"—another ritual we've included in meals since they were old enough to talk.

Our Sabbath includes a meal, whether it's a Saturday evening welcoming Sabbath or a Sunday evening reprise. As I said, sometimes we have other friends or neighbors join us. During the summer, we usually spend part of the weekend at my in-laws' lake home, so we enjoy a meal with extended family.

If you don't ever have family meals, that might be the first step on your Sabbath Simplicity journey — to try to have one or two family meals during the week. That might be the first revision you make — to eat somewhere other than the car, to look into the eyes of friends or family and just stop to connect.

Kids actually love rituals. They provide a sense of safety and predictability. Kids love to celebrate, and many rituals are celebratory, or ought to be. If you don't believe me, try changing the family traditions you have around the Christmas holidays or a small child's bedtime routine. What rituals can you make a part of your week, not just for their own sake but for the bonds of love they will create, for the sense of security they will give your family?

prepare for worship

For many Christians, Sunday is a day to go to church, not just for worship but for board meetings, committee meetings, and other obligations. The day is full of religious activity, but not rest.

Individuals cannot change this alone, but together, they can begin to question the status quo and change their churches. After all, a church is not a building but a body of believers. And if enough people want change, they can facilitate that change. But first, churches must see the importance of rest and allow it.

Do the words "go to church" and "restful" go together in your mind? Why not? The Sabbath begins at sundown. At that point, what are you doing to prepare your heart for worship? Gathering for corporate worship adds meaning to a day of rest.

Again, preparation is key—perhaps setting out church clothes the night before, having a coffee cake or other simple breakfast food ready to simplify getting out the door.

At one church where I led a retreat on slowing, simplicity, and Sabbath-keeping, women confided to me that volunteers at their church were rarely given any time off. They wondered how they might apply the things I taught in an environment of Christian workaholism. The one week the choir director decided to let his volunteer vocalists take a week off, he was chastised in front of the congregation for slacking off.

Many churches schedule committee meetings and other obligations for members on Sunday afternoon, which leaves little time for families to rest and reconnect with each other. This is often a reaction to how busy church members are during the week. Sunday is the only day they have time to meet.

One way to breathe life into your church is to work in teams so that the same people don't have to put on the service every week and so that more people can participate. Of course, this assumes that the church empowers and invites people to use their gifts so that the work of ministry is shared, rather than carried by only a select few. If your church is resistant to that idea, you've got some praying to do. You will have to ask God whether you should stay and try to change your church or find a church that supports your effort to make Sabbath a day of both worship and rest. Maybe you just need to learn to set some boundaries, to say no to the requests that make Sunday another working day. A church that believes every person has some role in the body is one that is likely to feel more supportive of Sabbath, because no one is doing all the ministry. Our theology and practice will affect our ability, as a church and as individuals, to keep Sabbath.

Some churches have a potluck meal at the church on Sunday evening, to provide both food and fellowship. This connects single folks with married people, creates a sense of family, and offers a respite from having to cook, since everyone brings just a single dish. My own church, which is quite large, encourages members to have Sunday evening or afternoon gatherings, called "the table," in homes, where members invite neighbors over for a simple meal and a chance to connect relationally.

Does your church help or hinder your efforts to keep Sabbath? If you think it hinders you, do you need to set clearer boundaries, or prayerfully consider finding a different church?

practical considerations

If you are going to change how you do Sundays, you'll have to change the rest of your week.

For example, I don't do laundry on Sundays, which means that I need to do it on another day of the week. Actually, one revision I've made this year is to stop doing everyone else's laundry. My kids are now in junior high, and they have been taught how to use the washing machine. So I launder my own clothes, and they do theirs. Even my husband has learned to use those big white machines (which, it should be noted, he operated quite efficiently for years while he was single). We no longer have those difficult conversations:

"Where's my blue shirt?"

"Hmm, I don't know. It might be in the dirty laundry."

"I wanted to wear it today!"

"I didn't know that!"

Not surprisingly, we don't miss those conversations one bit. We each have a day of the week when we're to use the washer and dryer, although we're pretty flexible about it.

I also make sure other chores are done before Saturday evening. That doesn't mean I do all the chores. Saturday has become a bit of a ritual day as well—we all help to clean up the house, and the kids each clean their rooms before they can play.

My parents both work, and on Saturday mornings, they go out for breakfast, then come back and clean the house together. My dad often puts on Fleetwood Mac or some other classic rock CD while cleaning, I guess to keep him moving as he's mopping or whatever. When we visit them, we join in. We go early to the pancake house, then help clean the house. (These are small rituals that the kids actually enjoy, although the pancakes are more popular than the cleaning.)

On a recent Saturday, the kids and I were cleaning the house. My daughter, thirteen, suggested we put on a Fleetwood Mac CD while we cleaned. Why not?

Sundays are much more restful if the house is clean. Clutter distracts, agitates, induces guilt if you sit down. When we're looking at a mess, it's hard to rest. So we all work together to make the space visually peaceful (not necessarily perfect) so that we can enjoy a day off without thinking we'll have to clean it up tomorrow.

Perhaps you grew up enjoying an elaborate family dinner on Sundays, which meant Mom or Grandma most likely spent part of her Sabbath working in the kitchen. My family often went out to brunch on Sundays, stuffing ourselves in preparation for a Sunday afternoon nap, then just had sandwiches or leftovers for supper. One family I knew had a hearty meal in the middle of the day but then enjoyed popcorn and apples for dinner so Mom could have a break.

I've chosen to revise: I usually don't cook a big meal. We sometimes have another family over and get carryout. Some folks object to eating out or even getting carryout meals on Sunday, since technically that's shopping and it also prevents your "servants"—the waitstaff and cooks—from being allowed to rest. Again, let God guide your choices. If you don't get carryout, someone has to cook—although leftovers are a good choice. Stouffer's lasagna and Texas toast is a favorite Sabbath meal at our house, because both prep and cleanup are unbelievably easy. Another strategy is to cook a little extra once or twice during the week so that you can have leftovers on Sunday. Or if you are the one who usually prepares meals, let someone else in your house prepare and clean up as a way of serving the family.

Again, a key part of practice is preparation, and nowhere is that more true than with Sabbath practice. Preparation includes everything from getting chores done to training your family to put in requests ahead of time. The ancient Jews were fastidious about this. They even designated Friday, the day before Shabbat, as Preparation Day. (Jesus died on Preparation Day, which is why he was hurriedly put into the tomb and why the women came to finish anointing his body after Sabbath.)

It might be helpful for you to designate Friday or Saturday as Preparation Day, a day to cook and clean but also to prepare your heart—and for those with children, to get organized for the coming week. For example, sometimes children procrastinate on school projects, which can result in tearful pleas for trips to Office Max on Sunday afternoon when they suddenly remember the project they must make for school, which is of course due Monday.

How can you avoid this? It will be painful, but only for a short time if you hold your ground. Communicate as clearly as you can. Warn your family (repeatedly) that you will not be running errands on Sunday. On Friday, ask the kids if they have projects and need any supplies so you can take them to the store to get them before Sunday. (Key: *take them.* Make them find what they need. Don't just go get it for them while they stay home and play video games.) Then on Sunday, when, despite your warnings and queries, they ask you to just run to Target or whatever, say no.

And don't cave in. *Just say no.* It may be painful, they may cry or cajole or curse, but if you give in, they won't learn. If they suffer the consequences just once, it's most likely they won't "forget" again. If you've warned them, follow through. This exercise will help in other parenting battles as well. Let your no mean no. If you give in just this once, you'll simply have to repeat the process over and over until you decide you've had enough. Decide now. You'll thank me later.

no, enough, and stop

As you attempt to revise your life, as you move forward in your Sabbath Simplicity journey, it will help you to learn three little words.

Part of why our Sundays feel so hectic is that we've said yes to far too many things. Our week is too full, and as a result, the busyness crowds over into Sunday.

Living at a slower pace overall will make Sabbath easier to keep. But it begins with saying no. You don't say no to everything, but use your no judiciously to keep your pace sane. Ask, "How will this affect my Sabbath?" before you say yes to anything.

Everything that fills up your Sundays right now is something you've somehow said yes to. You may have been pressured, you may not have thought it through, but your time is taken up each day by things you've agreed to.

Sometimes you've said yes for very good reasons—you want to keep your job; or you want to be a good adult child, so you say yes to visiting your mom in the nursing home. Some yeses should be a part of your schedule, even if they're not what you'd choose, because they stretch you toward God and build your ability to love others.

If you have several children and you've said yes to their requests to play a couple of sports each, then you have, by doing so, said yes to busy Sundays even though you may not have thought about that when filling out the form for Little League.

There's a fine line here, and only you can determine where to draw it. Activities are often a healthy part of a child's life, but too much activity, especially if it involves intense competition, can be detrimental.

Because of many temptations teenagers face, especially when they have too much free time on their hands, many of my friends with teens keep their kids busy. And I applaud that, within reason. But rather than keeping them busy for the sake of being busy, try to steer them toward meaningful activity.

My seventeen-year-old niece, for instance, swims on a swim team, and when she was younger, she sailed competitively during the summers. She's a great student and puts a lot of time into her studies and often does volunteer work in her community as well. This summer, my sister-in-law, in a chance conversation with a doctor, found an opportunity for Lindsey (who aspires to be a surgeon) to "job shadow" a surgeon (accompanying him not only on rounds but into the operating room) one day a week during the summer. Is she busy? Yes, but she's also gaining some meaningful experience as well.

Teens often find themselves short on sleep because their internal clock shifts. They don't just enjoy staying up late; they are hardwired, apparently, to do so. They need some downtime for naps or just lounging.

Preschoolers, on the other hand, need much more unstructured play time than we tend to give them.

Kids of any age need time with their families, but quality

time with a six-year-old will look different from time bonding with your teenagers.

If you say no to overscheduling during the week, you'll find your weekends are much less hectic. Saying no brings tremendous freedom because it opens up the opportunity to say yes to things that really matter. Like having time to pray with your spouse or play with your kids.

If you say no to things that sap your energy, you can say yes to things that bring you joy, that truly matter to you. You may simply have to list all the things you are doing—we often don't realize how much we have taken on—and then decide which things you enjoy and which things drain you.

A friend of mine always responds to any invitation or request for her time with this simple sentence: "Let me get back to you on that." She never says yes or no right away, even if she thinks she is certain what her answer will be. This lets her check her schedule, pray about commitments, and talk it over with her husband, but it also buys her some time. How many times have you said yes to something (such as serving on a committee) and later regretted your quick assent?

It's not nicer or better to say yes, because every time you say yes, you're saying no. Saying yes to one thing means you've said no to alternatives. Choose your yeses carefully.

Learning the word *enough* will also simplify your life. If you have enough stuff, you have less clutter to contend with, reduced need to shop for more stuff, and fewer worries about losing things. How much is enough activity? Just sitting down with your family to discuss that question would likely take you far on your Sabbath Simplicity journey.

How much stuff is enough? We often shop as recreation, but we end up burdened by more stuff. Then we need to spend time managing, organizing, and storing that stuff, or getting rid of other stuff to make room for the new stuff. If you feel overwhelmed, weighed down, you'll find great freedom in saying, "I have enough." A great way to begin a Sabbath Simplicity journey is to decide you will not shop on Sundays. Revise your identity from being a consumer to being God's beloved child.

As I've pointed out before, the Hebrew word Shabbat means "to stop, to cease." We'll examine that in more detail in the next chapter.

5

pausing

A Retreat from Our 24/7 World

*Our bodies move to a rhythm of work and rest that follows
the rhythm originally strummed by God on the waters of creation.
As God worked, so shall we; as God rested, so shall we.
Working and resting, we who are human are in the image of God.*
—Dorothy Bass, *Receiving the Day*

"So, do you work?" I think no question irks me more when it
is directed toward moms. Especially when directed toward me,
truth be told.

Every mother is a working mom. I have friends who seem
to live a life of leisure, involving a lot more tennis and shopping
than mine. But even at-home moms have families to care for
(sometimes handling both young children and aging parents),
households to manage, meals to prepare, errands to run, decisions to make.

The website Salary.com estimated in 2007 that if a stay-at-home mom were compensated for all the elements of her "job" — from housekeeper to CEO — her salary would be $138,095. An article on Salary.com notes, "Salary.com found the job titles that best matched a mom's definition of her work to be (in order of hours spent per week): housekeeper, day-care-center teacher, cook, computer operator, laundry machine operator, janitor, facilities manager, van driver, CEO and psychologist. New job titles that made the list in 2006 include psychologist, laundry machine operator, computer operator, and facilities manager."[1]

Most moms don't get much sleep. They seem to be so busy that they never stop. They seem to work without ceasing.

Our lives are meant to be lived in a rhythm of work and rest. I think for many women, a barrier to Sabbath is not seeing the value and importance of their work. "I'm just a mom," they'll say. "I'm just a housewife." (Does anyone use that word anymore?) Still, even if we don't say it, we think it. If we don't see the things we do each day as important work, we're less likely to think we might need to take a day off.

Many women I know work as secretaries or bookkeepers for a family business or handle all the investments, bills, and record-keeping for their households. When you ask what they do, they often say, "Oh, I just help keep the books for my husband's company." No offense, guys, but if a man were doing that same job, he'd proudly answer the same question, "I'm the chief financial officer of a privately held company!" I'm not faulting men in this; I think women ought to learn to value their work enough to answer the same way.

Ironically, because we don't think of what we do as work, we never stop working.

The closest translation English offers to the rich Hebrew word Shabbat is "to cease." The word implies not passivity but a decision to refrain from our work, our efforts, our busy-ness—not just coasting to a sputtering stop but stepping off the treadmill even as it continues to move. To cease is to take a stand against the tyrant of urgency, which boldly decrees that everything is top priority. In stopping, perhaps we will see the impossibility of that really being true—everything cannot possibly be top priority all at once.

When we Sabbath, we cease from our labors and from a lot of other things. We choose to pause, not just momentarily but long enough to put down our burdens for a time and rest in the arms of a God who not only encourages and refreshes us but offers to carry our burdens with us. To keep the Sabbath holy means to set it apart, to make it different from the rest of our days.

Jesus invites us to "learn the unforced rhythms of grace" (Matt. 11:30 MSG), to dance through life, or in it, rather than rushing headlong past it. To move in balance, gracefully. Even a sprinter has a rhythm, a balance. Sabbath Simplicity is a sanely paced, God-focused life. Our pace is determined not by the length of our to-do lists but by whether we pause (and for how long) between the items on those lists. Our focus is determined by what lies at the center of our lives. Many of us feel life is chaotic, without balance, without meaningful structure. An essential element of rhythm, structure, and balance is the pause.

a basic rhythm

When my children were young, we took music classes together through Kindermusik,[2] a wonderful method of combining music with play. Some of the early classes introduced the idea of rhythm—a series of beats either sung, clapped, patted on knees, or tapped with sticks or bells. Often the teacher sang a pattern and the children (with their parents, when they were toddlers) sang it back. Children learned note names simply by singing them. "Seeee, aaayyy. See, see, aayy." In the same pattern, the children would sing the note names on pitch. The children didn't realize that they were singing middle C and the note two below it, A, and that they were singing two measures of quarter-time music and were learning-by-doing that two quarter notes equal a half note. The teacher never lectured, only demonstrated. First, they had to learn the rhythm and how to mimic the sounds the teacher made. To them it was just a game. Yet the concept of rhythm teaches us, without our realizing it, more than we know.

Our life with God is meant to have a rhythm, a cadence. God demonstrated that rhythm in creation and again in the life of Jesus. When we read his story in the Gospels, we see that he fully engaged, even to the point of feeling tired. He regularly sought the refreshment of solitude, time alone with his Father, but he did not spend all his time in reflective silence. He spent a lot of time with all different kinds of people. His life had a rhythm punctuated by meaningful pauses. He engaged fully, then rested. He moved purposefully between service and solitude. He often was busy but knew when to pause.

So how do we establish a rhythm? Where does one go to "learn the unforced rhythms of grace"? Well, Jesus invites us to walk with him, to watch him and learn from him. But perhaps we're wondering how to translate the life Jesus lived, in a different era, a different culture, into our sometimes chaotic lives.

My kids and my twentysomething friends will often remark, when something doesn't make sense to them, "That was random." If someone says something that doesn't fit in the conversation, or if something odd happens, that's the observation: "That was so random." God is not random, but we live in a world full of randomness. We're often bombarded by things that don't make sense, things that don't fit.

What makes rhythm? Not just random pounding or shaking a bell nonstop. Not silence, either. As my kids learned in their music class, the combination of engaging and pausing creates a rhythm. If we were to clap on the first and second beats in the first line of a song, and the first and fourth in the next line, we'd have lost the rhythm. Yet our postmodern lives have us clapping randomly, without pattern or sense. And we can't figure out why we feel so off kilter.

We must learn the rhythm that God has wired into us, and to begin, we must pause.

Pausing is difficult because it seems so simple. It is the space in between — the white space between the words on a page, the rests between notes of music. But without the space, beauty gets lost. Meaning is much harder to discern.

Pausing, ceasing, brings sense to life. A pause, a bit of space, creates a break in the action. But pausing does not mean never going again. The spaces between help us discern the meaning of the words. We need to stop but then move again. Rest, work, rest, work. Breathe in, breathe out.

And while we're called to Shabbat, to stop, once a week, pausing is a practice that will bring sense to our lives if we practice it more than once a week.

our daily routine

Depending on your season of life, your day may have a structured routine or it may feel quite random. The more children you have and the younger they are, the more absurd and unstructured life may seem.

Does your day have a rhythm or pattern? Do you include rituals in your day? How much time do you spend doing the various tasks that fill your day? Do you even know? Do you have any margin in your life — room for the unexpected? I don't know about you, but I can pretty much expect something unexpected in every day. Which negates, in part, its unexpectedness, I suppose. But do you have some extra space in case things don't go as planned?

You may find it helpful to keep a time journal. I work from my home, except when I travel to churches or retreat centers to speak (about two times a month). When working at home, I would write for a while, then go downstairs to toss in a load of laundry or take a break to run an errand or, truth be told, go play tennis for an hour or two.

But last year, I felt like I was always working. So I decided to keep a time journal in which I wrote down what I did and the times I did it. So it might say,

8:00 a.m. to 10:00 a.m.:	writing
10:00 a.m. to 11:00 a.m.:	exercise
11:00 a.m. to 1:00 p.m.:	Target, grocery store, lunch in the car, dry cleaner's

And so on. On the advice of a friend, I decided not to do housework while writing. I chose to treat my writing like a real job and do the chores when I finished working for the day.

I was surprised to learn that what I'd thought was a little freelancing on the side was taking thirty hours a week or more. I also realized that I spent more time checking email than I really needed to. No wonder the house was a mess!

Try keeping a time journal to figure out where the time goes, and then take a look at it, perhaps even with a trusted mentor or friend. Do you schedule breaks? Do you have some margin for interruptions or emergencies?

Some of us appreciate, even need, structure. We like to plan, to prepare, to schedule. Others like to take life as it comes and get bored and even frustrated by a routine.

Most times, if someone loves structure, they will end up

married to someone who doesn't. Trust me on this; I speak from experience.

Whether you live by your to-do list or simply make things up as you go along, you'll benefit from pausing. If you are highly structured, you may have to plan to pause. If you're very unstructured, it will just happen, but you can let go of feeling guilty about letting yourself get off task for a while—it's healthy!

I discuss this idea in my book *Breathe*: "Pausing is not the same as collapsing. Some people say, 'I'll do all my pausing at the end of the day, after the kids are in bed.' That's not hitting the brakes; that's running out of gas. Both get you stopped, but only one is intentional. And only one will help you feel more rested and peaceful."[3]

In earlier chapters, we talked about fully engaging and fully disengaging. Just to clarify, fully engaging is not the same as multitasking. The term multitasking was coined to describe computers that are able to run more than one program simultaneously. And while it's an asset for a machine to be able to multitask, it's not optimal for human beings. Although we often feel like we're getting more done when we multitask, it actually erodes our efficiency while increasing stress.

If you find your kids are hanging on you, whining, keeping you from getting anything done, you're a typical mom. And your kids are normal. But often we respond to this kind of situation by yelling or deciding we need to keep the kids busier. These aren't always the best solutions.

My friend Tahna struggled as a new parent. Her son, Hudson, was a colicky baby. Now that he was two, he sometimes acted willfully and stubbornly (in other words, normal for a two-year-old). His angry outbursts alarmed her, and because he was her first child, she felt uncertain as a mom. While it is perfectly normal for two-year-olds to be feisty, she was looking for ways to parent him more effectively.

She had the opportunity to hear Jack Groppel, a human performance expert, speak at a conference. Groppel said that "multitasking is the enemy of the extraordinary" and suggested that rather than doing many things at once, you break your day into chunks.[4] During each chunk or period of time, focus on just one thing, even if it's only for twenty minutes.

"I realized I never did one thing at a time," Tahna writes about the experience. "I would multitask. Always. And when you are multitasking, nothing, and no one, gets your full attention, not even God, not even yourself."

Around the same time, Tahna read in 1 John 3:1, "See what great love the Father has lavished on us, that we should be called children of God! And that is what we are!"

"The word 'lavish' stood out to me," she says. "It surprised me, because lavish implies extravagance. I'd never thought of God's love that way before. I realized that I wasn't doing that—lavishing love—with anyone, not Hudson, Greg [her husband], God, or myself."

Tahna decided to focus first on receiving God's lavish love. As she did that, God filled her and strengthened her, and that strength empowered her to lavish love on her family. While it's not easy to find time to spend with God when you have a two-year-old, Tahna got creative. Sometimes she found peaceful quiet time for the day in the bathtub after her little boy was tucked into bed.

As she focused on God's love for her, she began to look for ways to let that love spill over into her family life. In her relationship with her son, Tahna decided to stop multitasking while she spent time with him, to lavish on him her full attention.

She writes, "First I set some boundaries: I told Hudson that I would play, fully engaged, with him for thirty minutes, and then I had to go clean the kitchen. I set a timer and set his expectations. And it worked. I didn't do anything else during that thirty minutes. After I played with him, he was okay with my leaving for a short period of time. Sometimes he would play by himself, and sometimes he said, 'I watch you clean the kitchen, Mommy.'"

Tahna also decided to try to turn Hudson's play ideas into activities that both she and her son would enjoy. Before being a mom, she had been a reading teacher. She got creative, which often happens when you slow down enough to gain perspective.

"While we built with blocks for what felt like an eternity, we took digital photos of our progress," she writes. "I made the photos into a book and then typed words that Hudson dictated to me. So now we have this great homemade book—that he can read—about the day we built a castle in our living room."

Pausing and chunking her time, focusing on one thing at a time, actually allowed her to get more done and to find more meaning and joy in what she did. She found she enjoyed her parenting role more and felt more confident in it.

"I was surprised to find that I had more energy and less stress. Even better, Hudson had fewer temper tantrums, came to lunch without a fight, and went to bed easier. It's like he had been trying to tell me all along, 'All I want is some undivided attention.'"

breathe in and breathe out

As we discussed in chapter 2, a daily rhythm of rest (sleep) and work is the foundation of Sabbath Simplicity. But even throughout each day, pauses are necessary.

Could you chunk your time? Focus on one thing at a

time? Lavish attention on someone you love, if only for a few moments?

Could you pause? Try this: next time you move from doing one thing to the next, take thirty seconds simply to sit still and breathe. Or if you work at a desk, stand and do a few simple stretches before moving to your next task. After a stressful meeting, take a short, brisk walk to clear your mind.

How are these related to Sabbath? Sabbath-keeping is about taking a break for a day. If you don't know how to stop for even a few moments, how will you stop for a longer period of time? If we are trying to run a mile, we may have to start by running shorter distances. What's true of running is also true of stopping: most of us are so used to always running in high gear that if we want to learn to stop and rest, we may have to practice. We may have to begin by just stopping for a little while, to build up our ability to do it.

Pausing is not just a chance for us to rest. It provides us the strength to be a better person. If we pause before we speak or before we act rashly, we may find it easier to act or speak as Jesus might.

Dr. Chuck Webber is a respiratory physiologist, a scientist who studies breathing. (That's a vast oversimplification.) He's a professor of physiology at Loyola University Medical Center in Chicago. Basically he's a scary-smart PhD, but he's a really nice guy. When I spoke at a conference at his church recently, Dr. Webber introduced himself to me.

We'd been talking about slowing and Sabbath, about catching your breath, from a spiritual standpoint. He pointed out that a normal breath consists of three actions: inhalation, exhalation, and pause, or to use the technical terms, inspiration, expiration, resting. The technical terms, ironically, are also the more poetic. As we breathe in, we inspire and are inspired—filled with the presence of God. When we expire, we die, unless we can take another breath. At each breath, we take only as much as we need for that moment. We breathe in and breathe out, remembering that God is as close as the air we breathe. But then, we pause. The pause, in a typical breathing pattern, is about as long as the inhalation and exhalation combined.

We often think only of inhalation and exhalation, but the pause is key.

Dr. Webber notes that the way to vary your breathing, to slow it down, is not by inhaling or exhaling faster or slower but by changing the length of the pause. It's in the pause that healing can occur. The pause, in a heartbeat, in a breath, is the most variable part, he explains. But generally the pause is as long as the inhalation and exhalation combined.

Dr. Webber has been learning lately about breath prayers, simple prayers that can be prayed in the space of a single breath. When I teach people about the breath prayer, I suggest that they combine a name for God (Lord, Savior, Friend) with a desire or a word of worship. But until I talked to Dr. Webber, I had not considered the pause. I had limited myself to breathing in God's name and breathing out my prayer to him.

"Here is my take on the breath prayer: breathe in (God's Spirit), breathe out (God's praise), pause (listen quietly for God's direction)," he says. So often we forget to pause. We forget to listen.

We think we are so busy we cannot take time to pause. But consider this: even your heart, which beats continually, rests. It pauses. When? Right after each beat. Your heartbeat has a rhythm—it beats, then it rests. That's how the heart, which is a muscle, can continue day and night. Because it pauses, or rests, every second, Dr. Webber explains, it can go for a lifetime. The key to endurance and strength is resting—not just once a week but on a regular basis.

What if when someone insults us (even behind our backs)

or we feel afraid, we were to pause? What if, rather than lashing out in anger or defensiveness, we were to stop, consider, remind ourselves to love? To listen quietly for God's direction. More important, to remind ourselves that we are loved, deeply. To pause, and then allow ourselves to be inspired, to breathe in God's love and truth. To remind ourselves that because of God's love, we have all that we need. The secret of loving is often found in taking a breath—in waiting, even for a moment. Again, the space is what creates beauty.

It's in pausing that we can receive gifts. If we run through our days and weeks, we run right past them. We do not receive what God wants to give because we never stop. Or we grab and glance, like a child ripping through Christmas presents, not noticing what treasures he's accumulating because he's focused on *how many* things he has rather than on *what* he has. And our hurry injures us because it injures our relationship with God. To not stop and pause and connect is to reject God's most precious offer—intimacy with himself.

Author Wayne Muller writes, "Our life is not a problem to be solved; it is a gift to be opened. The color of the sky, the song of a bird, a word of kindness, a strain of music, the sun on our face, the companionship of friends, the taste of sea air, the shape of clouds in summer, the reds of maples in fall—there are so many gifts in a single life. If we are preoccupied with what is missing and what is broken and wrong, we lose the miraculous harvest of all these tiny gifts, piled one upon the other, that accumulate without our acknowledging them."[5]

Pausing is countercultural and, for many of us, counterintuitive. It is a way of standing up to our culture's message that everything should keep running 24/7. Pausing gives us freedom from that unrealistic and unhealthy way of life.

So how do we find ways to rest, like tennis players between points, during the game of our lives? Small changes can have great impact. Stopping for a few moments to focus on something else can refresh us, even if the pause is the result of an interruption.

blessed interruptions

I am writing on a summer afternoon. My son is at the pool with friends; my daughter is at a friend's house. Through my open window I hear some of the younger neighborhood children in my front yard, talking to and petting my dog, and then, a moment later, knocking on my door. I walk downstairs.

"Ms. Kent, we can't find our parents," they say, quite seriously. "The cars are in the driveway, but we looked and we can't find them."

My house is one where kids are welcome, and the neighbor kids know it. "Are you sure?" I ask. "Did you look for them?"

They assure me that they've searched their homes to no avail. I slip on my flip-flops and walk out into the sunny afternoon to find the missing caregivers.

"Aren't your parents at work?" I ask Trevor and Delaney, brother and sister.

"Yes, but we can't find our grandma," they reply.

"There's a couple places we didn't look," says their friend James, in all seriousness. "We didn't check at Dairy Queen." I assure him that we don't need to ride our bikes the three blocks to Dairy Queen to find his mom.

In a moment, I spot James's mother and Trevor and Delaney's grandmother sitting together in James's back yard, which, because the house is on the corner, is in plain view of my front door. "There they are," I say, calling to the two women. The kids and I cross the street together, and the mom and grandmother point out that they've been out on the patio the whole time. We share a laugh but also tell the kids, "You did the right thing. If you can't find your mom or your grandma, go and tell a neighbor and they'll help you."

This little adventure took perhaps five minutes. But it provided so much: a short rejuvenating break from staring at the computer, a few moments in the sunshine, a chance to laugh and connect with my neighbors, a chance to affirm to the kids and my neighbors that we are here for each other and that they can find help when they need it. Pausing, even unexpectedly, added texture and richness to my afternoon. It gave me a chance to feel grateful for my neighbors and the way we help each other, and provided a story to share with my husband and kids at the dinner table (and with you on these pages).

What if I'd told the kids, "Go away, I'm busy writing a chapter on the value of pausing"? I think even the five-year-old would have caught the irony of that.

If you have a bit of margin in your day, you can not only pause, but you can enjoy the pauses and allow them to feed your soul, to rejuvenate you. Simply by stopping for even a minute or two, you can begin to recover your life. By being interruptible, you can open yourself to the gifts of God, to the presence of the Spirit in others and yourself. In your workplace, in your church, in your family—are you open to the gift of interruptions?

Interruptions are opportunities for spiritual growth. In the Gospels, we see that Jesus was often interrupted. And yet he responded with love. He paused, noticing not only the person but the truth behind their story and the divine opportunity in the interruption.

How do you respond to interruptions? The next time you are interrupted, choose to believe that it's God's way of telling you to pause.

Sabbath is just one type of rest, and it's a good one. But if we are used to running full speed, stopping for an entire day might be overwhelming and seem impossible. Pausing is a practice that can train us to rest, even for five minutes—to try stopping, just a little, to learn how lovely it is; to pace ourselves, to build up our ability to rest so that Sabbath will not seem so jarring.

ceasing

In her excellent book on Sabbath, Marva Dawn writes that Sabbath is primarily about four things: ceasing, resting, embracing, and feasting. And yes, ceasing is different from resting. Ceasing is pausing, choosing not to do what could be done. When we cease our work, we make space for God and his love, and for sharing that with others.

"To celebrate God's love on our Sabbaths also transforms us so that we can more deeply value others in the same way," Dawn writes. "When we are not under the compulsion to be productive, we are given the time to dwell with others, to *be* with them and thereby to discover who they are."[6]

Dawn outlines various things that Sabbath calls us to cease from—not only work, productivity, and accomplishment but also anxiety and worry.

Sabbath is a spiritual practice, and as part of that discipline, we must decide to cease from worry and anxiety. How do you do that, exactly? Well, you'll have to experiment a bit. I find I am less anxious if I prepare my home for Sabbath by clearing away the clutter. I am not a neat freak; I am very comfortable with a bit of mess. My office has piles of books and papers all over both desks and the floor, sticky notes and papers taped to the walls, and tote bags with various books and papers hanging over the back of the chairs. Someday I will straighten it up. Maybe.

Still, I appreciate a tidy space, because clutter creates not only visual distraction but reminds me of all the things I have ceased from, things I have left undone. On Sabbath, I don't go into my office. Other parts of my home are much less cluttered. I spend the day before Sabbath cleaning up a bit, quieting the voices of the undone chores by doing them ahead of time. Several women I interviewed for this book said they spread out the preparation for Sabbath over several days so that it's less stressful. Such practice makes sense—it's once again that "three days to prepare, three days to reflect" rhythm that has been a part of ancient Sabbath traditions.

We can also ask God to help us stay calm and peaceful, giving our anxious thoughts to him throughout the day as they come up. When we do so, we find that "Sabbath is not a running away from problems, but the opportunity to receive grace to face them."[7]

being at home

Sabbath-keeping is deeply connected to our homes. As I've mentioned, in the Jewish tradition, Queen Sabbath is welcomed not in the temple but in the home, not by a priest but by the woman of the house.

When the Jews have been persecuted, scattered, their synagogues burned, their people killed—still they have kept Sabbath, and as the saying goes, it has kept them. It is a spiritual home, of sorts. When they did not have a sacred space to call their own, they found refuge in a sacred time.

Our culture, unfortunately, is losing its understanding of sacred time. What were once holy days (the root of "holidays") are now seasons of overconsumption filled with pressure to buy things we don't need. Likewise, we are slowly forgetting how to sanctify our homes, to make them sacred spaces. Perhaps that is because we spend so little time in them. For it is time spent in a space that makes it sacred.

In 1970 the size of the average home in America was 1,400

square feet (a cozy three-bedroom, one-bath ranch or flat). In 2004 it was 2,330 square feet. That's a pretty significant jump. I have several friends who have homes that are double or triple that average size. My own home is larger than that average. Unfortunately, the costs of those homes also have skyrocketed.

The ironic part is that the average number of people in the American family has declined, and it seems to me, the amount of time we spend in our homes is also declining. We've got bigger homes, with fewer people living in more space, we're spending a lot more money on them, but we're not spending any time in them.

Still, according to a national survey, 94 percent of Americans say "home is the most important place in the world." The survey, done by budget furniture-seller IKEA, also said that despite that, we don't spend much time in the kitchen: 38 percent of the respondents said they spend only eleven to twenty minutes per day in the kitchen. Not coincidentally, it seems, 46 percent of those surveyed said they spend more time at work than at home.[8]

According to that same survey, 44 percent of the respondents said they always eat on the couch, and 26 percent eat takeout food two or three times per week. No wonder the traditional Sabbath practice of gathering for a home-cooked meal around the table feels so countercultural.

Not far from my neighborhood are several upscale subdivisions where McMansions sprout like so many mushrooms. The owners of some of these homes are rarely in them, since both spouses have to work more than full-time to afford the mortgage and property taxes on their fancy houses.

Of course, we've got bigger cars too, and we definitely are spending time there!

If we were home most Saturday nights, Sabbath would be an easy discipline. When people ask, "So what are you doing this weekend?" they often seem to be referring to where we are going: out to dinner or to the movies or on a weekend trip somewhere. But it is possible to have fun without going out and spending money. A simple meal together, time spent reading or playing board games together, taking a walk or bike ride with family or friends—these are ways to have fun and relax. Part of Sabbath-keeping, perhaps, is to reclaim these activities as part of our spiritual practice.

Others of us find that soccer games and errands and activities disrupt our best intentions for Sunday afternoons. If only we didn't have such busy children or such long to-do lists, we could truly rest on Sabbath. Again, what we say yes to all through the week will affect what our Sundays are like.

On a recent Sabbath, I sat with my feet up on the couch, in front of the fire, reading a book. I had a fleece blanket my daughter had made for me over my knees, Mozart playing on the stereo, and a cinnamon-stick candle burning. My thirteen-year-old wandered in, sniffing appreciatively the smells of candle, fire, and home. In the course of our brief conversation (she knows I am interruptible on Sundays), she remarked, "My friends like our house. They say it's cozy." I love that. My modest, sometimes cluttered, not updated house feels cozy to the teenagers. I may have the original kitchen cabinets, but my daughter's friends feel welcome. That, to me, is worth a lot and is a picture of what it means to live your priorities.

A few Sundays ago, life was not quite so idyllic. Scot was working, and the kids bickered, mostly because my daughter was nagging her brother. I sat down with my daughter and had a little chat about what it means to provoke someone. She explained that she thought she was helping me, nagging him so I would not have to. I'm guessing this might be a typical firstborn trait. I probably did it for my mom.

But we had the time to chat. I really tried to listen, which is easier if you are not thinking about other things you have to do. And that's the gift of Sabbath—it's a day when you have all the time you need to listen because you have banished your to-do list for the day. I did not have other things to do. I did not have to say to Melanie, "I don't have time right now to discuss this." How often do we say things like that, promising to talk things over later, and we never do? Sabbath allows us to be fully present, to live in the moment, even in difficult ones.

So that Sunday, I had time to guide and teach my daughter. We talked about how to sandwich constructive criticism between two positive comments to make the correction more palatable. I instructed my daughter in conflict resolution, in discernment. I tried to shape her strong will and leadership gifts in a way that honors God and still honors who he made her to be.

Often, during busy weeks, we have to have conversations on the fly, in the car, or for a few moments at dinner. But on Sunday, I have all the time I need to listen and to chat with my kids. I'm a better parent on Sunday.

Later that day, we went swimming at the pool, and the kids played together happily, somehow reconciled, at least for the time being. To see my daughter teaching her brother to dive and the two of them tossing a ball around and playing together was rich.

That night, at Melanie's suggestion, we had "breakfast for dinner"—bacon, eggs, and toast, an easy Sabbath meal. Later, we played Scrabble until the two of them were giggling and making up words. I didn't insist on finishing the game. I didn't chastise them for being silly. I delighted in their giggles and fun.

The seasons of life in which Sabbath-keeping seems impossible are the seasons you need it the most. Your children need to see you rest and to know that it's okay to stop achieving, running, and doing for a little while. One of the most important developmental skills you can give your children is the ability to daydream. You can't sign them up for a class on it. You can't direct them in how to do it. You have to give them, as small children, enough downtime simply to discover it on their own. Conversation with you and reading books, interspersed with time for daydreaming, fosters brain development and neural connections much more readily than watching videos.

You can facilitate this with very young children by continuing a daily nap time, even if they don't sleep. During that time, they must be quiet and on their beds (no video games or music). They can read or just lay down and relax. Several families I've spoken to told me their Sabbath practice includes Sunday-afternoon naps for everyone in the family.

What we must regain, if we truly want to keep Sabbath, is the knowledge that we have choices, and the courage to make them.

basking in grace

God loves you unconditionally. He has, as we pointed out earlier, lavished his love upon us. But God is not indifferent about sin. Like a good parent, he's pleased by the behavior that is good for us in the long run and saddened by behavior that ultimately hurts us. God wants the best for us, so he can honestly hate what we do when we act rebellious, but he's able to love *us*, even when he doesn't like what we do. God's love for us is not altered by our mistakes.

His rules are not arbitrary but are in our best interests. His command to rest, for example, is not capricious but one that restores us, physically and spiritually. It's an opportunity to bask in God's grace. Sabbath truly is a gift from our loving parent. But like cranky toddlers who resist a nap, we often fight against what is good for us, what heals us.

Sabbath, however, offers more than just a nap, a chance to chill. In taking some time to rest, we are not only healed and refreshed; we have an opportunity to experience the truth of God's unconditional love. We can say, "God loves me no matter what," all we want, but if we are always working, striving, running, we don't experience that truth, live in it.

A few years ago, I attended a prayer meeting. Gathered in a circle, we each talked about where we'd seen God at work in our lives that week. One of the men said he had set his alarm one day, planning to awaken early enough to pray before he went to work. When the alarm awoke him, though, he struggled to get up. He considered rolling over and simply blowing off his prayer time so that he could sleep longer.

"I realized at that moment," he said, "that God loved me the same whether I got up and prayed or went back to sleep. That realization—knowing he loved me that much—made me want to get up and spend time with him."

God loved him the same whether he got up or slept? Really? This truth somehow threw me off balance. I had said, "God loves me unconditionally," before then, but his story offered me a concrete example of what that means. It took me a little while to absorb the truth of his story.

God loves you the same when you work hard and when you do nothing. But if you never do nothing, if you're always doing something, how will you really know, experientially, that God loves you when you're not working or when you're not busy?

That's not to say we should never work. The Bible tells us to rest on one day but also makes it clear that we are to work the other six days. However, that work does not earn God's favor.

Think about last Sunday. Did you have time to rest? Moments just to enjoy the people God has put in your life or to relish some time alone? When you are just relaxing, do you feel guilty? Bored?

The cry of our hearts is to know that God loves us no matter what. Sabbath answers that cry because it creates space for us to do nothing, space God's love can flow into.

the sacramental ordinary

In liturgical Christian traditions, the church year consists of two main festivals: Easter and Christmas. As one of my favorite lectionaries explains, "From the beginning the Christians celebrated Easter as the anniversary of Jesus' resurrection. The Season of Easter lasted seven weeks, culminating on the day of Pentecost, which celebrated the giving of the Holy Spirit to the apostles."[9]

These two holidays (holy days) are preceded by the seasons of Lent and Advent and end on Pentecost and Epiphany, respectively. But between those seasons of celebration, those days set apart, the calendar is filled with weeks that are not holidays. The church calendar refers to the seasons after Epiphany and after Pentecost as "ordinary time."

The only holiday during ordinary time is Sabbath. On that day, many Christians remember the resurrection by taking communion and gathering with the body of Christ. "For Christians, each week's Sunday was, and is, a 'little Easter.'"[10]

I once interviewed literary scholar Devin Brown about C. S. Lewis's classic Chronicles of Narnia. A professor of English literature at Asbury College, Brown has written about how both Lewis and, even more notably, Lewis's friend and colleague J. R. R. Tolkien loved what he calls the "sacramental ordinary."

In a paper on Tolkien, Brown writes, "Tolkien's trilogy is filled with scenes of great moment — events such as the colossal battles fought at Helm's Deep and the siege of Gondor. However, at the same time Tolkien places an equally strong focus on the value and the significance of the commonplace of this world, a focus on what could be called *the sacramental ordinary* in Middle-earth.... It is likely that Tolkien acquired some of his sense of the sacramental ordinary from his reading of Chesterton, who once wrote, 'Ordinary things are more valuable than extraordinary things; nay they are more extraordinary.' "[11]

Lewis was also intrigued by the commonplace, Brown told me. He said one of the most magical aspects of the books is Lewis's ability to infuse everyday occurrences with a sort of quiet spiritual wonder. In *The Lion, the Witch, and the Wardrobe*, for example, Lucy goes through a wardrobe to find herself in a magical land, where it is winter. She meets a faun, Mr. Tumnus, who invites her back to his cozy little cave for tea. So in the midst of this fantasy story, the narrative catches its breath. Despite the strange surroundings, Lucy and Mr. Tumnus pause to have a lovely time just chatting as they enjoy afternoon tea together. It is a moment of sacramental ordinary.

The story of the incarnation is one of sacramental ordinariness as well, if you think about it. The Son of God, born in a dirty, obscure stable to a poor teenage mother. To anyone who didn't know better, it would have seemed an ordinary moment.

Sabbath, at its heart, is really a moment of the sacramental ordinary. You may wonder, "If I'm home and I'm not doing housework, what will I do? Sit around and watch television?" Well, perhaps. Growing up in Chicago, I often by necessity spent Sunday afternoons mostly indoors in the winter. I remember watching *Wide World of Sports* sometimes on Sunday afternoons. Sunday evenings usually included *Mutual of Omaha's Wild Kingdom* and *The Wonderful World of Disney*. (This was in the days before you could pop in a video for the kids and before the Discovery Channel. I think Sunday television provided my mom a bit of Sabbath respite; if we were watching a Disney show, she'd get some uninterrupted time to read or relax!)

While it's sometimes fun to watch a football game in the afternoon or *Extreme Makeover: Home Edition* on Sunday night, television is not restful. It's a way sometimes to veg out, but it doesn't reenergize you. Often on Sundays I read—sometimes a spiritually challenging book or maybe some poetry, and sometimes just the Sunday *Chicago Tribune*. I do encourage the children to read or to play outside. The best way to encourage your children to play outside or to read is to model it. Get outside: garden, take a walk or bike ride, play with your dog (if you have one) or your children (if you have them) or friends (I hope you have them). Even in winter, you can build a snowman or take a short walk. Reading aloud, whether you have children or not, is a great way to connect with your family.

Because, by definition, sacramental-ordinary moments are not accompanied by hoopla, we can miss them. They're usually unplanned, serendipitous. But we're more likely to have them (or notice them) if we create the right conditions for them, if we open ourselves to the possibility for them. We need to create some space for God to show up in our day.

That may mean making sure that somewhere during Sabbath, you share a meal with your family, that you choose to be available to the people you live with, that you make a phone call to extended family who may live far away. It may mean turning off the computer and the television to be fully present rather than distracted.

We think we need rules, but in seeking them, we miss the divine in the ordinary.

Author Mark Buchanan writes,

> This is maybe the primary mistake we make when we try to figure out the Sabbath: We go straight to the rules. What can I do; what can't I do? Can I garden? Shop? Play football?

This is the pharisaical tendency, to concoct rule upon rule and, in a mechanical, dutiful way, try to fulfill them. In Jesus' day, the religious leaders had buried Sabbath keeping beneath a thick crust of strict and finicky regulations. They'd lost the gift beneath their lists.

Jesus repeatedly broke their rules for just that reason. He wanted to shock us into the awareness that keeping Sabbath is not about keeping rules, it's about recovering God's heart, His passion and compassion, His desire for people to be all they were created to be.[12]

Sabbath-keeping may look different in different seasons. For me, living in Chicago, Sabbath in winter is vastly different from Sabbath in summer. That's why flexibility and freedom are an important part of this practice.

Three seasons of the year, I find myself puttering in the garden on most Sunday afternoons. This may mean I'm weeding, pruning, harvesting, or digging. It may mean I'm sitting in my plastic lawn chair, just resting and admiring the flowers, watching the birds or bumblebees. The garden is also a place, though, where I am imminently interruptible. My children know that they can talk to me when I'm gardening.

One Sunday, I pruned the pink rose bush in my garden. My dog, Jack, lay on the grass in the sun near me as I puttered at an easy pace. Rose pruning can be a spiritual experience if you let it. It requires attention and yet allows your mind to wander. I often pray while pruning. I never hurry through it.

After I removed the spent blooms, I sat down in the grass next to the dog, enjoying the sun. I scratched Jack gently behind his ears and looked up at my roses. The sky, September blue with a few whispery clouds, provided the perfect backdrop. I sat looking at the roses against that blue for a good fifteen minutes, studying them like you would a Monet in a museum. I grabbed my camera later and got a few great shots. Just enjoying my roses was a luxurious gift. When else do I have that kind of time?

Sabbath offers us a chance to rediscover the lost art of puttering. In some ways, puttering is wasting time. You may not be able to waste a whole day, but could you set aside, say, an hour or two on Sunday afternoon just to goof around, to do something that brings you or those you love joy? Could you take a break by doing something that is simply fun without a lot of pressure to produce some result? In doing so, you may find yourself tumbling through an unexpected portal into a place of the sacramental ordinary.

When you putter, you may find that you actually are, without intending it, being productive. That's okay. I think Jesus often healed on the Sabbath because he wanted to push us to examine the attitude of our hearts. Sabbath is a tool for us to use, not a taskmaster for us to capitulate to.

When I garden, I do accomplish something, although I am mindful to move at a leisurely pace. But really, none of my gardening chores has anything to do with getting my daily work done. None of them puts words on the page, money in my bank account, or food on the table (except maybe when I pick the tomatoes or zucchini). When I garden, I am not answering email, lining up speaking engagements, writing an article. Pruning or weeding may require me to exert myself, but it doesn't earn me a penny and, in fact, pulls me away from my earning a living. And yet, in a strange way, taking time to get away from the computer and the phone renews me so that come Monday, I am more productive than I would be if I had not taken time.

It's an interesting phrase: to *take* time. Rather than having it taken from me or feel as if it is slipping through my fingers, I take time, like the gift that it is. By taking time to rest, to pause, to look into the faces of my children and at my roses, I receive joy. I take hold of time, embrace it, play with it. In so doing, I recover the joy that I thought I'd lost. I enjoy it, relish it.

Sabbath time is a gift, one that we can play with. What does that mean, to play? To be playful? That is what we will consider in the next chapter.

6

playing

An Escape from Workaholism

Play is subversive, really. It subverts business as usual.
It subverts necessity. It subverts utility. It subverts all the chronos-driven,
taskmaster-supervised, legalism-steeped activities that mark out
most of our lives—that make us oh-so-useful,
but bland and sullen in our usefulness. Sabbath is for play.
—**Mark Buchanan,** *The Rest of God*

Have you ever seen one of those videos, designed to tug at your heartstrings (and purse strings), showing the plight of children in a third-world country? Often interspersed among the images of hungry, dirty waifs crying in their porridge, you'll see another shot of children playing. In ragged clothes, they kick a patched soccer ball on a dusty bit of ground, make mud pies, sing to a tattered doll, play tag, or simply scamper about. Despite the pain of their lives, or perhaps as a way of coping with that pain, something in them compels them to engage in play.

Children, even those seemingly robbed by poverty of any semblance of a childhood and facing horrific circumstances that make them grow up too fast, are hardwired for play. A group of children with a bit of time on their hands, without instruction, will invent a game. My children learned games from other kids on the playground or invented their own. No adult taught me how to play tag as a child, but I spent hours playing it. I learned it from the kids on my block, in its endless variations: freeze tag, flashlight tag, dodgeball, SPUD. Tag, unfortunately for the health of our children, seems to be out of vogue these days, but children still love to play.

What does it mean for grown-ups to play? Do we outgrow playfulness? If so, is that a good thing?

For a while, one Sunday a month, we joined several other families from our neighborhood and had a Sunday-evening game night. Kids from preschool through high school, and their parents, all played together. In the summer, we usually played kickball. All the grown-ups participated. Everyone brought food and we picnicked after an hour of games. In winter, we rented the gym at the Park District building for an hour, playing dodgeball or funny relay races or a game in which you chase people and when you catch them, you have to join hands until you form a huge human chain chasing the last few who have not yet been caught. After gym time we went out for pizza.

Game night provided a great way to get to know our neighbors and have fun, just to goof around and laugh. But play goes beyond just hanging out—games offer both flexibility and structure, teamwork and individual effort. When people play together, it strengthens relationships (sometimes by testing those relationships when we have to work out conflicts). On those family play nights, the conversation over dinner was always lively, I think because play breaks down barriers, encourages cooperation, and builds relationships. It's easier to talk to people after you've laughed with them, allowed yourself to be a bit silly with them.

Children are playful. What does it mean to play, to be child-like (which is a bit different from being childish)? What did Jesus mean when he said that the greatest in his kingdom were those who chose to be like little children (see Matt. 18:1–4)? Did he want us to be playful? Does that mean we all ought to play more dodgeball? Why did Jesus say that's important? Or was he talking only about humility?

"There is no mistaking that one must learn to resemble a child in order to enter the kingdom," writes Brennan Manning. "But to grasp the full force of the phrase 'like little children,' we must realize that the Jewish attitude toward children in the time of Christ differed drastically from the one prevalent today. We have a tendency to idealize childhood, to see it as the happy age of innocence, insouciance, and simple faith. In the Jewish community of New Testament times, the child was considered of no importance, meriting no attention or favor. The child was regarded with scorn."[1]

Manning notes that a humble attitude allows us to see God's grace for what it is: pure gift. But how do we cultivate humility? It's not easy in our culture, which lauds individual opinions and accomplishments, which teaches that self-esteem and self-confidence are of the highest value. But I believe playfulness is a path to humility.

While we may have a different perspective on childhood than Jesus' contemporaries did, he continues to call us to trust him. And to realize we're not "all that." Play stretches our ability to be a fool, to engage in that which has no purpose other than simple joy. Play forces us to loosen our grip on our ambition for a while; it trains us, almost subversively, as Buchanan says, in humility. We often want to avoid the risk involved with being silly. It's odd, since Jesus said we ought to be humble, that

Christians especially seem to find it difficult to let go of our self-importance and image management.

Play is something most of us have forgotten how to do, but it is necessary to restore our souls from the damage of our accomplishment-driven, workaholic culture. Play is a spiritual practice and a key part of Sabbath-keeping.

If you are married, do you play with your spouse? If you have children, do you play with them? Simply relax and giggle and laugh with them? Play board games with them?

When my children were small, I didn't necessarily enjoy board games because of the mind-numbing quality of games like Chutes and Ladders or Sorry. Don't get me wrong—I like certain games, especially Scrabble or Taboo. Little kids' games just challenged me in ways I didn't enjoy. In spite of my distaste, I would force myself to play Candyland with Melanie, though sometimes I'd stack the deck so she got Queen Frostine and won as quickly as possible. (Oh, come on—admit it, you've done the same thing. Or you are secretly wishing you'd thought of that.) At the time, I even saw it as a spiritual exercise designed to cultivate patience and forbearance: the discipline of Candyland.

But now that my children are older and their interest in playing with me is beginning to get crowded out by other interests, I find I'm much more open to kicking a soccer ball in the yard or playing Monopoly or another board game with them.

play gets lost

As a society, it appears that we are putting a lot of time, energy, and money into destroying play, even for our children. Or at least convoluting it into work whenever and however possible. I play tennis in a league with a bunch of other middle-aged women. You'd be amazed at how many of them seem bent on making a career out of it, investing time, energy, and money at a frantic pace.

Kids "play" soccer, baseball, lacrosse, or whatever else their parents sign them up for, but these sports seem to have become a business, which costs money (especially if you are in a more competitive travel league or on an elite team). Some children play video games, which do more damage than good, in my opinion, and certainly offer none of the health benefits of tag.

In fact, most kids and parents use the word *do* rather than *play*, it seems. "Billy does football in the fall and hockey in the winter," we'll say. We don't say our kids are going to play a game; we say they "have" a game. As in have to, as in have an obligation, an item on their to-do list. Rather than playing games, our kids have things to do. Though we may use such language unconsciously, our word choices are stunningly accurate.

We live in a neighborhood where I can actually send my children outside to play, and we know our neighbors well enough that everyone looks out for the kids. While they don't have the freedom I had as a youngster to be gone for hours on end, I definitely give them more opportunities for independence than other parents I know.

We also don't have video games at our house. Often my son will want to play with the boy next door, and I will remind him to play outside. Because otherwise, even on a beautiful summer day, they'll end up inside, engaging with the Xbox.

Do you know how to play? Often adults engage in sports, but it is with a sense of competitive intensity. Many people who are immersed in sports do so only as spectators of professional sports. They won't miss a game, but the only exercise they get is jumping off the couch when their team scores. Can you imagine the impact on the overall health of Americans if we learned to play? If the millions of people who watch *Monday Night Football* spent as many hours engaged in playing sports as they do observing them?

Many adults who exercise see it as drudgery rather than play. Or it becomes an obsession, a god they compulsively sacrifice large amounts of time and energy to. They don't play for fun; they exercise in an attempt to look younger, to stave off the inevitable aging process. Or it becomes a stimulant, another addiction. Rather than just enjoying a game of catch with the kids or a walk through the woods, we feel the need to engage in extreme sports.

"The rhythm of life for countless people ... emerges as one that oscillates between driven achievement (both on and off the job) and some form of mind-numbing private escape," writes Tilden Edwards. "This crazed rhythm, based on a distorted view of human reality, increasingly poisons our institutions, relationships, and quality of life."[2]

This "crazed rhythm" is not play at all. True playfulness brings joy; it teaches us trust. We can believe God is able to keep the universe humming right along without our help. Play is truly an act of trust, and trust is a key part of childlikeness.

Many adults like to "party," but that word has lost much of its playful connotation and often is just a form of that "mind-numbing private escape" Edwards writes of. Even though people party together, the word has become a euphemism for drinking alcohol (or using other substances) for the purpose of escaping problems or just trying to fit in socially.

Most adults I know have forgotten how to play. The joy has been squeezed out of them, and their hearts have been damaged as a result. Our accomplishment-driven, workaholic culture destroys souls. When I speak with high-achieving individuals, I often hear them talking about their work as a means to an end, a way to gather some money and some stuff, but the joy will come when they retire (as early as possible) so that they have the time to enjoy it. I sometimes hear them say they'd like to do something more significant with their lives than just work, but they're unclear on what that could be.

Sabbath is a spiritual practice, of which play is a quintessential part. In play, we shed the shackles of schedules, efficiency, even purpose. The playfulness of Sabbath is the key to its ability to restore our souls.

chronos and kairos

Rabbi Abraham Heschel's famous treatise on Sabbath points out that the practice of Sabbath creates sacred time. While temples, churches, and even certain beautiful places in nature are what we may call sacred space, Sabbath sanctifies time.

"The meaning of the Sabbath is to celebrate time rather than space," Heschel writes. "Six days a week we live under the tyranny of things of space; on the Sabbath we try to become attuned to holiness in time."[3]

The ancient Greeks distinguished between two types of time. *Chronos*, or *kronos*, named for the Greek god who swallowed his children, is linear time, chonological, measured, logical. How apt a picture of our driven society—our playfulness swallowed and destroyed by our busyness. What we keep careful track of with watches, clocks, and calendars is chronos (clock) time. And though we seem to control it by measuring its minutes, hours, and days, it does seem to threaten to swallow us up, to keep us running in fear and anxiety.

But a second word, *kairos* (pronounced "ky-ros"), has to do with those moments when we lose awareness of the ticking clock. It's when we are in the moment, when time passes and we are unaware of it. It means "at this moment" but also "the fullness of time." Like Sabbath time, it is sacred time.

Interestingly, the New Testament, which was written in

Greek, makes much use of this distinction. Specific moments in history when God steps in are considered kairos moments.

Joseph Tkach and Neil Earle write,

> *Kairos* refers to specially selected periods of divine determination. It operates within profane human time but mainly as the focus of the fulfillment of God's ultimate purposes.
>
> When Jesus came the first time it was a definite *kairos* moment—a time of fulfillment, a time of judgment and a time for God's promises to become operative (Mark 1:15; 2 Corinthians 1:20).
>
> Note this from the book of Titus: "Paul, a servant of God and an apostle of Jesus Christ for the faith of God's elect ... [in the hope of eternal life,] which God, who does not lie, promised before the beginning of time [Greek *chronon* from *chronos*] and at his appointed season [*kairos*] he brought his word to light" (Titus 1:1–3). God created time, and in his sovereign *kairos* time he interacts and enters into *chronos* time according to his perfect will.[4]

Have you ever engaged in something that you so enjoyed that you lost track of time? Something fun or absorbing? Something that didn't have a point or a purpose, other than itself; something you did just for the fun or interest or excitement of it and you forgot about yourself and your to-do list? In other words, did you ever just play? In the losing track of chronos time, we touch kairos time.

Having a deep conversation with a dear friend, reading an absorbing book, or engaging deeply in some creative endeavor can usher us into kairos time.

Those impoverished children I mentioned have discovered a truth that all children instinctively know: play is a path to kairos. Their impromptu games allow them to live in kairos, to escape the cruel chonros of too many hours since their last meal and before the next.

The other day, working on this chapter, I decided to write for an hour but soon lost myself in studying and trying to understand these concepts well enough to write about them. I suddenly looked at the clock and realized an hour had passed and I needed to get my son to a birthday party on the opposite end of town. I was jolted back from kairos time to chronos. The rest of the day was chronos-driven. Or just driven, in the minivan. Driving my son to that party, my daughter to a friend's house across town, then back to run an errand, pick up my son, then my daughter. No more writing, no more research. No more thinking, pondering, creating. No more art, losing myself in the writing process. Only chauffeuring, which I am still trying to find a way to make into a creative enterprise.

A hobby like knitting or scrapbooking (so I'm told) can put us in kairos time, can be playful, if you let it. If we long to experience kairos time, we can begin by learning to play. Play often opens up time in a way that allows us to shed the chains of chronos.

Madeleine L'Engle writes,

> Kairos. Real time. God's time. That time which breaks through chronos with a shock of joy, that time we do not recognize while we are experiencing it, but only afterwards, because kairos has nothing to do with chronological time. In kairos we are completely unselfconscious, and yet paradoxically far more real than we can ever be when we are constantly checking our watches for chronological time. The saint in contemplation, lost (discovered) to self in the mind of God, is in kairos. The artist at work is in kairos. The child at play, totally thrown outside himself in the game, be it building a sand castle or making a daisy chain,

is in kairos. In kairos we become what we are called to be as human beings, co-creators with God, touching on the wonder of creation.[5]

If playfulness puts us into kairos, if it somehow loosens the grip of our demanding schedules, then it is an appropriate and indeed helpful part of our Sabbath practice.

Abraham Heschel reminds us, "The Sabbath was given to us by God for joy, for delight, for rest, and should not be marred by worry or grief."[6]

putting this in real life

If you think you could never take a whole day to rest, then start smaller. Consider the possibility that you will make a journey toward a more restful lifestyle, that it may take some time to move forward on that journey, that recovering your life may require you to make some changes, some decisions.

A person who is, say, fifty pounds overweight and not at all fit cannot lose all that weight and become healthy just by declaring her intentions. She must make some changes, slowly, over time, and must sustain them. She will move toward health by deciding to move, to exercise, starting perhaps with just a walk around the block or a beginning exercise class. Crash dieting won't work—at least typically it won't last. Gradually changing unhealthy eating habits with better choices will make this person more healthy. Replacing the potato chips and soda with fresh veggies and water will help. Eventually, she will, if she's patient and persistent, recover her health. She may never be an Olympic athlete, but she'll be healthier.

The same is true for someone who is learning how to slow down, to rest, and even to play. Screeching to a halt rarely works. Just as with our physical health, trying to make too drastic a change will result only in discouragement, and ultimately we'll give up.

You do not have to be an Olympic-level Sabbath-keeper. The Sabbath was made for people, Jesus said. It's a tool you can use to become healthier spiritually — more connected with the God who loves you, more peaceful, more joyful. Not perfectly any of those things. Just healthier.

The path to Sabbath Simplicity for a busy family often begins at the trailhead of play. Do you have times for just having fun, for family meals, for taking walks, or for exercise that's fun?

I'm often surprised when I ask women, especially those my age or older, "What do you like to do?" and they don't know. So many of us are so deeply entrenched in the work of caring for others that we don't even know ourselves well enough to know what would be fun for us, if we had the time to do it. Younger women know what they like, but they are frustrated that they think perhaps they can't do those things because they are too busy.

What is play for you? What's fun? Do you even know? One thing I enjoy that is playful and restful for me is gardening. Now, if I worked as a landscaper, gardening would be work. But for me, I truly believe "we are nearest God's heart in a garden," and it brings me joy and pleasure to putter in my garden.

My husband, Scot, loves sports. An ideal day off for him in the summer sometimes includes what we jokingly call "a gentleman's triathalon" of sailing, golf, and tennis. I also enjoy activity, so I will often join him in two out of the three. (Sorry, golf is not fun, restful, playful, or even bearable for me!) In the winter, he's content just to watch sports on television. I'm not as into that, but it can be fun as well.

Does recreational activity re-create you? What rejuvenates you? If you had some time to do something you enjoy, what would that be? If you don't know, then perhaps the journey toward Sabbath Simplicity will begin for you with this simple question: What do I love?

One family I know sometimes takes their small children for a walk through the neighborhood, and they pray for each neighbor as they stroll past their home.

When I was growing up, my family would often take bike rides or go on walks together. It's not complicated. You just walk out the front door and walk around the block. This is a small step toward learning how to rest—doing something together that just relaxes and rejuvenates you, gives you an opportunity to talk to each other.

At first, you may have to schedule these things. To have a family meal at least once a week, to schedule a time for your family to go bike riding together. You may have to decide to leave some things undone or simply to be at home on Sundays instead of running errands.

One of the challenges while writing a book on Sabbath, especially as the deadline approached, was to practice what I preach and not write on Sundays. A few weeks before this book was due, I felt a lot of deadline pressure. But I dared myself to live the thing I am asking others to live. I found that the sweetest Sabbaths were those when I refused to let the pressure of an approaching deadline keep me from living the life I am asking others to consider.

I occasionally had to get creative. My son had been asking to go to Chicago's Museum of Science and Industry, where we have a membership. It's an amazing place. So on a Sunday afternoon just a few weeks before the book was due, I took Aaron and a friend to the museum to see the visiting exhibit on Star Wars, his all-time favorite movie series.

I chose that day to connect relationally with my son, to get out of the house so I wouldn't be tempted to work. For months, he'd been asking to go, and I'd always said, "We will soon, but I'm really busy."

Visiting a museum is a great way to play, especially when it has a lot of interactive exhibits, as this museum does. Since we already have a membership and we brought sandwiches to eat in the car on the way to the city, the trip cost very little. I spent a few dollars on parking and even fewer on coffee for myself and a snack for the boys.

If this appeals to you, I'd suggest getting a membership — pick one place per year to join. This takes the pressure off of having to see it all in one day to get your money's worth. It provides incentive to go, since you've already paid for it.

If wandering a museum sounds boring, then that's not your kind of play. That's fine. You have freedom to play in whatever way God made you. Ask yourself, What would I enjoy? What would my family (or if you are single, my close friends) enjoy doing with me?

If your family is resistant, start with the only person you can control: yourself. Explain to the people you live with that you will not be working on Sundays, and find an hour or two for yourself. Play. That may mean physical exertion. It may mean doing needlepoint. It may mean wandering through a museum. Do what you love, and enjoy the gift of time.

one family's story

Ginger Garrett works from home as a writer, and when I interviewed her, she was promoting two new books, editing a third, and writing a fourth. She'd started practicing Sabbath a few years earlier.

"I kept hearing people talk about Sabbath; I think I heard someone preach on it, and I felt like God was challenging me to try this discipline," she says. "There's a Chinese proverb that says if one friend tells you something, you can ignore it, but if two friends tell you the same thing, it's God talking."

Ginger and her husband, Mitch, have three young children. (When we spoke, the kids were ages six, five, and two.) The Garrett family started slowly with their Sabbath practice. "I would turn off the computer on Saturday night and not turn it on again until Monday morning," Ginger says.

That may sound simple, and it is, but having the computer off allows you to do other things—to give attention to the people you live with, to take a nap, to enjoy freedom from having to check email or work.

"Now we're working on turning off the TV," she says. Ginger's Sabbath practices demonstrate two key principles: (1) start small, start anywhere, but start, and then (2) seek to grow in the practice.

During the week, the family is always up early, by 6:00 a.m., Ginger says. If she's facing a deadline, she'll get up super early, sometimes as early as 3:00 a.m. Not surprisingly, she describes herself as a type-A personality. But because she works hard in the mornings and while the kids are at school, she doesn't work once they get home. Her rhythm of work and rest is not only weekly but daily.

"We knew we needed to find a way to rest," she said. An interesting side effect of keeping Sabbath has been that both Ginger and her family find that because they've made a habit of resting on Sunday, they find themselves feeling tired that day. "We used to have the same energy level pretty much all week," she says. "Now, we're tired on Sundays. More often than not, we'll conk out on the couch." But because they can rest without feeling guilty, their energy level is higher on Mondays.

Sabbath at the Garrett home is a day of freedom but also is one focused on God. "It's become a day of not entertaining, not cooking, not reading stuff I'd normally read," Ginger says.

"I'm reading a Eugene Peterson book on Sundays lately that is much deeper spiritual stuff than I can read while waiting in the carpool lane."

Sabbath has become a day of rest for her family. Because their children are small, Ginger and her husband use the day to connect with their kids. Often that means playing, which is not always easy for busy people to engage in. Often rest is a discipline.

"Sabbath is a seed that you plant, and you have to let it grow and change as it will," she says. "You just have to get the rocks out of the way of its growth.

"One large rock we're trying to move right now is that we are trying to focus on doing things as a family on Sundays. This week, that meant doing Slip 'n' Slide with the kids for three hours. Well, my husband was out there for a while, and I took a nap, but then I went out and did it with them. I'd actually rather do housework, but it's something I force myself to do. As a type-A person, I have to make myself be totally relational on Sundays. A verse in Proverbs says 'no discipline seems pleasant at the time,' but the benefits are amazing."

In other words, sometimes play is a discipline. Play is a means to connecting relationally, which is part of what Sabbath is about.

Still, Sabbath is "a moving target," she admits. "It changes as your life changes. I'd like to have a blueprint that doesn't change, but that's not how it works. It's an organic process, one that will change with the seasons of life."

Sabbath refuels Ginger's creativity.

"It's the day I do the least, and yet it feels like the most productive," she says. Ginger says that as a writer, it feels like she's always having to come up with ideas and words. On Sundays, as she plays with her kids, takes a nap on the couch, spends time just hanging out, she says, "I get flooded with ideas. Usually I don't even write them down. Then they have a full twenty-four hours to marinate in my brain.

"When I get back to work Monday morning, I have a clear overview of the week, and I'm very clear on what is the priority. It saves me so much stress and anxiety," she says.

Ginger's two historical novels are set in the First Temple period—from the eighth to the sixth century BC.[7] In her research for the books, she learned that the Israelites used special perfume and incense that was for use only in the temple and the tabernacle. The house of God had a smell all its own, by design. "The part of the brain that registers smell is right near the part of your brain that handles memory. That's why a smell can evoke a memory, and you can be transported back to another place or time, even before you can figure out exactly what the smell is," she says.

Ginger loves candles and usually has one burning in her kitchen. But she decided to get a special candle that she would burn only on Sundays so that the Sabbath would have a scent all its own in their home.

"It's just one more way to put me in the frame of mind for Sabbath," she says. "I light it when we get home from church."

Looking again to Jewish history, the incense and smoke in the temple symbolized prayers rising to God, she says. "It speaks to me of the intangible nature of prayers and faith. It's a ritual that gives me a sense of the sacred."

The family attends North Point Community Church, a large seeker-friendly church in their hometown of Atlanta. Like many megachurches focused on reaching out to the unchurched, North Point's services are not liturgical. They don't have many rituals. That's fine with Ginger, but it has stirred her desire to create some rituals at home.

One ritual is breakfast. Her husband, Mitch, makes homemade waffles or pancakes each Sunday. This provides Ginger a respite from her cooking duties and allows Mitch, who works during the week as a computer consultant, a bit of creative fun.

People often ask how they can "do" Sabbath with small children, but the Garretts actually find it easier. Their young children are not in sports or other activities, except her son's Cub Scouts, which is a once-a-month obligation.

"I want margin in our lives. I'm not going to put my kids in anything until they're begging for it," she says. "Sometimes that makes me feel like a slacker mom, but the payoff is worth it. We have less hurry, less stress."

If your kids are already overbooked, your first step may be to take a look at their schedules and decide as a family which activities you might be able to drop.

seasons

What does your family's life look like on weekends? Does it vary from season to season?

As I've said, we're different in soccer season. But even then, we usually have church in the morning, a soccer game in the afternoon. We're only rarely traveling to a tournament.

In summer, the rhythm of our lives shifts. Many weekends, we go to my in-laws' home, located on a small lake in Wisconsin, about an hour away from our home. When our children were little, Scot's mom would delight in playing with her grandkids while Scot and I would sail—an amazingly rejuvenating activity. We found that for us, Sabbath needs to include recreation, that recreational activities truly do re-create us.

Sailing puts Scot and me in kairos time—we focus on the task, what the boat requires at each moment, not on how slowly or quickly time is passing. No schedule dictates which ropes to pull or where to steer, how to balance the boat; we must respond to the wind, to the boats around us (to avoid collisions), to the waves. The only chronos-driven part of the race is the starting sequence. A horn blows, a flag is raised, and we have exactly five minutes before we are allowed to cross the starting line. Cross it one second too soon and the race judge will make you circle back. Cross it too late and your chances of getting ahead of the pack diminish considerably. So I wear a stopwatch to time the starting sequence. As we jockey for position along an imaginary line in the water from the judges' boat to a buoy forty feet or so away, I call out a countdown so Scot knows how close to steer the boat to the line. But once we are across the line, and the starting horn has blown, we do not look at the watch again. We're racing not against the clock but against the other boats, and for the joy and exuberance of it.

When we visit my in-laws, we spend part of the day floating on rafts near the dock, but out on the boat, we're competing in races. Often the competition is fierce and the work of sailing extremely physical. Usually an afternoon on the boat draws us closer together, but sometimes we get into an argument about the way one or both of us made tactical errors. So is sailing work or play?

My daughter plays soccer in a league that has games on Sundays during part of the year. So when she plays competitively, is it play or work?

For us, the question we've used to make decisions about what's helpful on the Sabbath is, Is it restful or is it stressful?

I've known many folks who say you should not participate in competition on a day of rest. Several generations ago, many Christians opposed any participation in sports on Sunday. My great-grandfather, for example, was an avid baseball player. He became a Christian when he met my great-grandmother. At one point, he had an opportunity to play minor-league baseball. But he turned it down because he would have had to play on

Sundays. His own family (who didn't share his faith) disowned him because of that decision. But he stuck to it.

But we've found that sports, whether soccer or sailing, can rejuvenate us in a way that few other things do — if we approach them correctly. Recreation can re-create us if we remind ourselves to see it as a chance to be playful.

Melanie loves soccer. What she doesn't like is my standing on the sidelines yelling at her, coaching her a bit too loudly. We found that the answer to the "is it restful or is it stressful" question depended not on whether she was playing an organized game or a backyard pickup game but on how we as parents acted on the sidelines. The quieter we were, the more her enjoyment increased. The more we smiled and the less we yelled, the more joy she found in the game. She could just be playful, even as she strove to do her best. Without parental pressure, the game became just that — a game.

My desire is for Sunday to be a day when we recover, when we do things we otherwise "don't have time for," like watching the snow fall outside a window or taking a walk together as a family. We turn off the computer, spend time in the garden, take some time to really listen to our children. We're trying to fit that into a real life.

playing frugally

One of the lies of our culture is this: fun costs money, and the more you spend, the more fun you will have. Rejecting our consumer identity means letting go of believing these lies.

A key part of Sabbath practice is to rest and play without spending money. Author Wayne Muller notes, "Sabbath is a time to stop, to refrain from being seduced by our desires. To stop working, stop making money, stop spending money. See what you have. Look around. Listen to your life. Do you really need more than this?... Spend a day napping and eating what is left over in the refrigerator; play a game with your children, take a walk, have a cup of tea, make love, do nothing of consequence or importance. Then, at the end of the day, where is the desperate yearning to consume, to shop, to buy what we do not need? It dissolves. Little by little, it falls away."[8]

When we begin to enjoy all that we already have instead of focusing on what we don't have, we move toward contentment. We become people who are more content when we stop, rest, play, because in those things, we find great freedom. We discover that like a loving parent, God revels in the joy of his children. We are unconditionally loved by God even when we are not working or producing. Again, this leads us to contentment, where all we desire is relationship, and God meets that desire in the gift of playful recreation.

As we play, as we just enjoy time together with our loved ones and with God, we cultivate gratitude. And on Sabbath, as on all days, it is good for us to express that gratitude to God and to include conversation with him in our day. So it is to the practice of prayer that we will turn our attention next.

7

praying

An Antidote for Self-Absorption

Sabbath frames our entire life, helping us set priorities and determine which of our activities and aspirations bring honor to God. So what is at stake in Sabbath observance is not simply that we manage to pause and refuel enough to continue on in our frantic and sometimes destructive ways. The real issue is whether we can learn to see, and then welcome, the divine presence wherever we are. Can we link up as servants of God's covenantal love and see in that service our unending joy?
—**Norman Wirzba,** *Living the Sabbath*

In her 2006 book, *Generation Me: Why Today's Young Americans Are More Confident, Assertive, Entitled—and More Miserable Than Ever Before*, psychology professor Jean Twenge writes that the generation she dubs Generation Me (those born in the 1970s, 1980s, and 1990s) are more self-centered, more disrespectful of authority, and more depressed than any generation prior. She blames the self-esteem training many Gen-X and Gen-Y kids received growing up for their unrealistic, almost narcissistic self-absorption. The ironic result of trying to help these kids feel confident is that they have come to value their own happiness over the common good, yet find themselves profoundly unhappy.

Twenge, who is a part of this generation herself, writes, "Television, movies, and school programs have told us we were special from toddlerhood to high school, and we believe it with a self-confidence that approaches boredom: why talk about it? It's just the way things are. This blasé attitude is very different from the Boomer focus on introspection and self-absorption: GenMe is not self-absorbed; we're self-important. We take it for granted that we're independent, special individuals, so we don't really need to think about it."[1]

Of course, the young people are quick to point out that they didn't raise themselves. The Baby Boomers, who were the first to be called the Me Generation long ago, became the parents so bent on teaching self-esteem that they forgot the importance of teaching basic competence. Generation Me's confidence is based not on accomplishments but simply on the fact that they exist. Twenge points out that while Boomers may have been self-absorbed, they still did everything in groups. Today's young people are self-important and don't really care what their peers or anyone else does or thinks. But they put themselves at the top of their priority list. Making yourself happy is the most important thing.

Internet phenomena like MySpace, Facebook, and YouTube are all icons of a self-focused culture in which almost anyone can convince themselves that "it's all about me."

In a follow-up study released in 2007, Twenge and four other researchers found that Gen Y (also called the Millennial Generation) is more narcissistic than earlier generations were at that age. The study compared responses of more than sixteen thousand college students on a survey called the Narcissistic Personality Inventory. By 2006, they said, two-thirds of the students had above-average scores, 30 percent more than in 1982.

"We need to stop endlessly repeating 'You're special' and having children repeat that back," Twenge told the Associated Press when the study was released. "Kids are self-centered enough already."

Many people argued with Twenge's findings, noting that the same generation is less likely to be drug-addicted or to commit a crime than previous generations, and more likely to volunteer for humanitarian causes. But when a generation raised on praise for "just being you" hits a highly competitive workplace where they don't give out ribbons for just showing up, it's a rude awakening for many of them.

Even our spiritual lives have become self-centered. I hear a lot of people talking about "my spirituality" or a need to believe in themselves. Our prayers can easily turn into whining or morph into affirmations by which we attempt to shore up our self-esteem.

A positive outlook on life helps open doors sometimes. Self-awareness and assertiveness can be positive traits. But as Twenge's subtitle suggests, all this self-focus has not made anyone happier. This generation, for all its "self-esteem," is also known for high rates of depression and even suicide. Part of the problem is that the media and all that positive thinking raised the expectations of this generation. When real life sets in and they realize that they might not end up being a rock star or a millionaire, they are understandably disappointed.

It's easy to point fingers at others, to talk about "those young people today" who are supposedly so much more selfish than other generations were at that age. But the Bible says that all of us have a wicked, selfish streak inside—one that wants to put ourselves first.

The antidote for our self-absorption and self-importance (which afflict not just young people but all of us) is the practice of prayer. Certainly it is possible to pray selfishly—I would venture to guess that the majority of prayers would fall into that category. When we approach prayer with a Sabbath Simplicity mindset, though, we are focused on God, and then on others. The traditional Sabbath prayers begin, "Blessed are *you*, Lord God," and not, "Please bless *me*, God." (Although it's perhaps not surprising that a book instructing people to pray a "bless me" prayer became a bestseller.)

Prayer is so much more than just putting in orders with God, talking about ourselves and our problems. Prayer involves praising God, confessing our shortcomings, and listening to God as well.

Prayer informs our Sabbath; it infuses it with holiness. Otherwise, the Lord's Day becomes "our day," simply time to take a break. While taking a break is a healthy practice, Sabbath calls us to so much more than that. On Sabbath, we stop. But we don't stop just for ourselves. We stop to remember and to observe. We stop to remember what God has done and that we are not him. We engage in, or observe, certain practices that connect our souls with God and with others.

To see the connection between prayer and Sabbath, we must expand our understanding of prayer. What is it? On a bad day, we secretly (or not so secretly) fear that prayer is not far from just talking to ourselves. If we limit our understanding of prayer to a narrow definition that includes just "talking at God" and little else, we will miss out on the richness and restfulness of Sabbath prayer. Some of us find prayer a chore, relegating it to our "should" or "ought to" list. When prayer becomes obligation, it feels like work. Then how can it be a part of our Sabbath practice?

Prayer includes not just words but our attention (listening) and then, most importantly, our action.

again and again

In some seasons of our family's life, we've begun Sabbath on Saturday evening by going to church to help with the children's program. We attend the main service on Sunday morning, but on Saturday evening, my husband leads a small group of junior-high boys, while my kids and I help out in the three-year-olds' Sunday school room.

Three-year-olds are fun, in part because they are no longer two-year-olds. They are verbal but completely unedited. "I think I just went potty in my pants," they will tell you without any hesitation. During the singing time, they will dance (okay, bounce up and down) and sing with wild abandon.

One week, a little boy named Joshua and I blew soap bubbles for a little while. Then I pulled him around the expansive play area in one of the plastic wagons. On one trip around the room, he noticed the brightly colored Little Tykes slide. "I'm going to slide," he said.

"Okay," I said.

"You watch me," he said, pulling me by the hand. "You sit right here and watch me." He pointed to a spot on the floor just a few feet away from the plastic slide. I dutifully sat cross-legged on the floor. He climbed the three or four steps up the slide, sat at the top, and looked at me expectantly.

"Ready, set, go!" I said. After he slid down, I offered a high five. "Good job!"

He stood for a moment, then looked at me with his index finger raised, like a professor making a point. "I'll do it again!" he said.

This went on for a good fifteen minutes. Each time, he'd announce his intention to do it again, and he'd run in a wide circle to climb back up. Sometimes other children would join in; sometimes he slid by himself.

He was enjoying the sliding, but it would not have been nearly as much fun if I hadn't watched him. He enjoyed my attention. And I gladly gave it. The delight that he found in it made me smile.

Sitting on the floor in the three-year-olds' room watching Joshua, I thought, "This is what prayer is—enjoying the attention of God." God watches and listens—what an amazing privilege. And more amazing, our delight in being with him makes God smile. But also, prayer is giving our attention to God. It is a conversation of mutuality, of paying attention to God and reveling in the attention God gives to us.

If we miss that second part and somehow think that prayer is only about God giving *us* attention, then we're in danger of the narcissism we talked about earlier. Prayer is not an end; it is a means to relationship. It's not just talking, hoping some deity somewhere might hear us. Rather, it is coming into, and living in, the presence of God—to speak, to listen, to receive love, and then to give our love back to God, who like any loving parent desires not just to give but to receive. Prayer brings us joy.

Praying is, at its heart, paying attention to God. It is a powerful antidote to our human tendency toward self-absorption. Praying is not necessarily reciting words but listening. It's noticing where God is at work and then—and this is a critical part—joining in that work through service, through giving, through loving. It is appropriate to do something to help the poor on Sabbath or to serve others (as we do in the three-year-olds' room).

That can be accomplished in many ways, but it requires that we create some space and pay attention. To live prayerfully is to live mindfully. To notice, as Elizabeth Barrett Browning writes, "every common bush afire with God."

If we are truly focused on God, then we are not focused on ourselves. We can live our lives as a prayer if we find a sacred rhythm of work and rest. To have a day of peace is part of praying, during which we are strengthened and rejuvenated. But what are we strengthened for? To do the work God has called us to do, not as drudgery but as a pathway to joy. Prayer is not passive but active. To give and receive love is to live a prayerful life, even if we are not in direct conversation with God. Sometimes prayer means figuring out where God is at work in the world and then joining in that work, as Henry Blackaby demonstrated so well in his book *Experiencing God.* To do the second, you must first do the first, and that requires restful listening.[2]

This type of listening is done not just in silent reflection but in noticing things as we walk through life. Where is God at work? Ask him to show you that as you go through your day. My friend Wendy lives not far from me. Most of the children at the public grade school her children attend are, like Wendy's family, rather affluent. However, there are a few who are bused in from poorer areas nearby. Wendy recently learned at a PTA meeting that a small group of kids come to school without having had breakfast—not by choice but because their families can't afford to feed them. Because the average family income for their school is quite high, the school doesn't qualify for a federally subsidized breakfast program. But Wendy and some other PTA moms were dismayed to learn that children in their suburban school might be hungry. So they are creating a program to offer a free breakfast at their school. Some families have dropped off breakfast bars and other healthy snacks for the principal to offer to kids she thinks might need them. They're working to set up a food pantry for school families. God's work began when someone noticed these hungry kids. Wendy's part is to join in by doing something to help. She's also trying to help her neighbors understand that poverty exists in suburbia, even if they don't notice it, and what is an appropriate way to respond to the needs of others.

sheltered by God

Wayne Muller writes, "One translation of the biblical phrase 'to pray' is 'to come to rest.' When Jesus prayed he was at rest, nourished by the healing spirit that saturates those still, quiet places. In the Jesus tradition, prayer can be a practice of simply being in the presence of God, allowing the mind to rest in the heart. This can help us begin one aspect of Sabbath time: a period of repose, when the mind settles gently in the heart."[3]

Another Hebrew word that can be translated "to rest" is *mishkan*, the word often translated in English as "tabernacle." While the roots of the English word point us toward a tent or building, the Hebrew word has a much richer meaning.

Manfred Schreyer, a pastor from Ohio, has a great ecumenical Christian website and blog. An article on the site by scholar Lambert Dolphin offers this insight: "*Mishkan* is related to the Hebrew word 'to dwell,' or 'to rest,' or 'to live in,' referring to the '[In-dwelling] Presence of God,' the *shekhina* (or *shechina*) (based on the same Hebrew root word as *mishkan*) that dwelled or rested within this divinely ordained mysterious structure."[4]

So God says, "Build me a tabernacle." It's not just a tent; it's an invitation to rest with God. To dwell together. By building a tabernacle for God, his people were, paradoxically, sheltered by God. They had a physical reminder of a spiritual reality: God is with us, wants to dwell with us, wants to rest with us. God is not just in one place but dwells among us, can move with us.

Dolphin adds, "The Hebrew word for a 'neighbor' is *shakhen*, from the same root as *mishkan*. The commandments for its construction are taken from the words in the book of Exodus when God says to Moses, 'They shall make me a sanctuary, and I will dwell (*ve-shakhan-ti*) among them. You must make the tabernacle (*mishkan*) and all its furnishings following the plan that I am showing you' (Exod. 25:8–9)."[5]

So the ideas of prayer, rest, and dwelling with God are all related. We invite God to dwell with us. We live in him. We rest in him. We dwell with him, are sheltered by him, in a house of prayer. And that tabernacle, that sanctuary, goes with us.

In fact, tabernacle and Sabbath are intertwined in the Old Testament text. In both the thirty-first and thirty-fifth chapters of Exodus, God offers instruction on building the tabernacle. And in both chapters, the Sabbath (*Shabbos*) command (*mitzvah*) is repeated in the midst of the instructions. Sabbath rest and God's dwelling place are inexorably linked. In the Hebrew tradition, the thirty-nine acts prohibited on Sabbath are the same thirty-nine that were needed to build the tabernacle.

These acts includes sowing, plowing, reaping, spinning wool, grinding, baking, lighting or extinguishing a fire, and so on.[6]

Prohibited acts are, again, acts of creativity. We cease from creating to remember our Creator and to remind ourselves that we are not him. We set aside our work, our routine, to enjoy the gift of time with God. For that is what Sabbath truly is: a gift of time.

Sabbath is not a place but exists only in time. It is a sanctuary, but not one that exists in space, in which we can dwell with God, rest with him. By setting aside a day for God, we create a tabernacle. In this way, Sabbath is a tabernacle of time. Rabbi Shraga Simmons writes, "Why does the Torah juxtapose building the Tabernacle with the mitzvah to observe Shabbos? Because Shabbos and the Tabernacle are one and the same. They are both links to a transcendent dimension. During the Jewish people's 2,000 years of exile from the land following the destruction of our Holy Temple, Shabbos served as our sanctuary, the place to restore and refresh our perspective in a world often hostile to Torah values. As it is said: 'As much as the Jews have kept Shabbos, Shabbos has kept the Jews.' "[7]

Shabbos — to stop, to rest. Tabernacle — to rest, to dwell.

Tabernacle—the house of prayer. Prayer—to rest. See the connection? Sabbath prayer is a prayer of presence, rather than intercession or supplication. Sabbath prayer brings us into simply resting in the presence of God. Sabbath is a day on which we know that we are not God. Sabbath is a tabernacle of time that we can celebrate no matter where we are. God's rest goes with us everywhere. We echo the poem-prayer of David in Psalm 131,

> *My heart is not proud, LORD,*
>   *my eyes are not haughty;*
> *I do not concern myself with great matters*
>   *or things too wonderful for me.*
> *But I have calmed myself*
>   *and quieted my ambitions.*
> *I am like a weaned child with its mother;*
>   *like a weaned child I am content.*
>
> *Israel, put your hope in the LORD*
>   *both now and forevermore.*

Psalms 120–134, which include, of course, this one, are labeled "songs of ascent." These are songs that were sung as worshipers walked up to the temple in Jerusalem.

Coming to the house of the Lord, the sanctuary, the tabernacle, David reminds himself and his listeners, we are going to God's dwelling in a state of rest. In the house of the Lord, the tabernacle, we are like a weaned child with its mother, not demanding anything, basking in our heavenly parent's loving presence.

Sabbath and prayer are intimately connected—a place to rest with God carved out of time. In a way, the physical tabernacle was simply a visible reminder of a spiritual reality—that God dwells with us.

When Jesus came, he dwelt among people. He used the

temple in Jerusalem as a metaphor for his own body. And he invites us to dwell with him, remain in him, live in him (see John 15).

Isaiah 56:6–7 says,

> *And foreigners who bind themselves to the* L*ORD*
>   *to minister to him,*
> *to love the name of the* L*ORD,*
>   *and to be his servants,*
> *all who keep the Sabbath without desecrating it*
>   *and who hold fast to my covenant—*
> *these I will bring to my holy mountain*
>   *and give them joy in my house of prayer.*
> *Their burnt offerings and sacrifices*
>   *will be accepted on my altar;*
> *for my house will be called*
>   *a house of prayer for all nations.*

It's interesting that again, in this passage, the ideas of Sabbath and the house of prayer are linked.

sacred space

God is with us no matter where we go because he is omnipresent—his presence is everywhere. God doesn't live in buildings. In his famous sermon to the people of Athens, Paul says, "The God who made the world and everything in it is the Lord of heaven and earth and does not live in temples built by hands. And he is not served by human hands, as if he needed anything. Rather, he himself gives everyone life and breath and everything else. From one man he made all the nations, that they should inhabit the whole earth; and he marked out their appointed times in history and the boundaries of their lands. God did this so that they would seek him and perhaps reach out for him and find him, though he is not far from any one of us. 'For in him we live and move and have our being'" (Acts 17:24–28).

So why did God ask his people to build a tabernacle? Because although God exists outside of time and space, we live within it. We are so attuned to the physical world that we can be affected emotionally and spiritually by our environment. Being in a chaotic and cluttered place can make us feel unsettled. And when we walk into a beautiful space, it can make us feel serene.

Do you have a sanctuary within your home? If you have a chair or a corner where you pray regularly, eventually your body will subconsciously recognize that space. When you go into that space, you will feel calmer.

More important, do you have a sacred space in your heart? Are you aware of the shekhinah of God, the presence that goes with you everywhere?

If we have practiced Sabbath for a while, the day itself becomes a sanctuary of sorts for us. At least that's been the experience of Kent Kingston, who shared his story with me.

one family's story

Kent Kingston grew up in the Seventh-day Adventist tradition. "Fifth generation both sides," he says, noting that his father, brother, and uncle are all pastors within that denomination. Kent and his wife, Miriam, and their two children live in Cooranbong, Australia, about an hour and a half north of Sydney.

As the name implies, Seventh-day Adventists celebrate Sabbath on the seventh day of the week—from sunset Friday to sunset Saturday. Their church community gathers for worship on Saturday morning. Kent and his family feel strongly that because the Bible says the seventh day is Sabbath, that is when it should be practiced.

"God asks us to worship him on his time schedule, not according to our convenience," he says. "Sabbath-keeping within the divinely appointed period is an act of submission to one who knows better, even if we don't get why Tuesday wouldn't do just as well. Even if you don't want to get hung up on the 'which day' debate, Sabbath observance is still a sign of submission to God. You make a firm decision to maintain Sabbath observance even if it is inconvenient to you. In doing this you are putting God first."

Kent is honest about his struggles to keep Sabbath and about how it can easily become a day that he and his family are busy with church-related activities. He's had many Sabbath days that ended up being rushed or filled with too much activity, especially because he sometimes helps lead worship or Sabbath school at his church. And getting ready for Sabbath often requires a scramble of preparation.

"Sabbath begins at sunset on Friday night," he says. "Leading up to that time there is a general rush to get everything ready for Sabbath—cleaning up the house, doing the shopping, and so on. Many Adventist workplaces close early on Friday in order to give employees time to do this preparation. In the summer months, Friday afternoons are doable; in winter, when the sun goes down much earlier, it's a mad rush sometimes."

But over the years, Sabbath-keeping has created a sacred space in his week and in his heart.

"When you've been keeping Sabbath since childhood, something happens in your brain at sunset on Friday when you realize the busyness of the week is over," he says. "A sense of calm settles on your mind and the muscle knots begin to unwind. The problems of the everyday are put on hold—bills, school assignments, work deadlines, renovation projects. And because you know you won't be dealing with any of these things for the next twenty-four hours, you just forget about them. It's the greatest feeling.

"Friday evening is a special occasion for the family. We usually have candles on the table for dinner and fancier food—including dessert (which the kids look forward to immensely). We don't do TV dinners much during the week, but on Friday night, definitely not. The focus is on the table and the family.

"To mark the coming of Sabbath, we also have a devotional time on Friday night. Seventh-day Adventists use the term *opening Sabbath*. This usually involves singing a few songs together, retelling a Bible story, reading a Bible passage or an impromptu Bible quiz. When I was a child, we always sang a hymn to open Sabbath—'O Day of Rest and Gladness'—and we recited by heart Psalm 32, which speaks of the joy that comes with God's forgiveness."

While Friday night is focused on family, Saturday is spent with the larger community. Church services and Sabbath school take most of the morning (at the Kingstons' church, from 9:30 a.m. to about noon), and it is a tradition for church members to invite other families home for Sabbath lunch after church. Other times, everyone brings something to share for a potluck lunch at the church.

"It's a great way to get to know new people. Lunch tends to stretch well into the afternoon and usually involves another fairly standard practice, the 'Sabbath afternoon walk.' After a big lunch, it's either a walk or the risk of ending up snoring on your friends' living room floor."

Kent says this particular practice is especially meaningful to him. "It's a way that Sabbath can be used to get in touch with the expressions of God's identity through his creation—the natural world. Of course any nature walk can achieve this, but a Sabbath walk on the seventh day of the week has an extra resonance with the Genesis account of God creating the world in six days, declaring it 'good,' and then resting on the seventh day. A Sabbath walk is a chance to declare God's creation good all over again. When we are mindful of this, there is a sense of an unbroken chain of Sabbaths stretching back thousands of years to God's original day of rest."

Kent says family and friends often close Sabbath with a simple prayer, and if they are enjoying spending time together, they may decide to continue hanging out by ordering pizza and watching movies on Saturday night.

"Having the support of your church community in Sabbath-keeping is a really valuable thing," Kent adds. "There is a sense of shared understanding and purpose, even though there may be individual differences in the details of how Sabbath is observed. It makes Sabbath activities more enjoyable when you can share them with people who are like-minded about the purpose and blessings of Sabbath."

In some ways, Sabbath offers a respite from worry and concern.

"Sabbath is a day of rest, in a psychological and physical sense," Kent says. "Don't worry about work or school. Don't worry about politics or current events. Don't do housework or paid work or homework. Leave the commercial world behind."

The Kingstons take the Adventist rules against commerce seriously and find that although it takes discipline to do so, it actually makes their day much more restful. "We don't go shopping on Sabbath, for groceries or for fun," he says. "From a political as well as a spiritual point of view, I value the opportunity to drop out of the commercial arena for twenty-four hours every week. I think it helps to keep perspective. Going noncommercial for a day requires some preparation — shopping beforehand, making sure the car has enough petrol, getting together some cash for tithes and offerings to be given at church (the only context in which money will change hands on Sabbath). And it can be uncomfortable at times. Like when a tradesman calls you and says he'll be around between 10:00 and 11:00 a.m. on Saturday to attend to the washing machine. Do you vaguely say that this is a bad time for you or do you get specific and explain about the importance of Sabbath to you and your family?

"In the end, keeping Sabbath is more a state of mind than a series of behaviors. If you do not carry out any commerce during Sabbath but think of nothing else during that period, have you truly rested? I don't think so. That's why I tend to spend my Sabbaths away from shopping malls and try not to look too carefully at the 'For Sale' sign on the car in front of me during the drive to church. There's a paradox to it: Sabbath resting involves mental discipline."

To focus on the things of God and not on our materialistic culture is a way of praying. Kent also finds that Sabbath leads him to a prayer of self-examination. "Someone once said that the unexamined life is not worth living. Sabbath provides an opportunity for that examination, particularly in a spiritual sense. Is my life in keeping with God's plan? Are my priorities right? Do I really practice the presence of God? Sabbath is like a weekly spiritual tune-up in this respect."

One thing Kent wrestles with is how to teach his children to keep Sabbath without coming across as legalistic or burdening them with a big list of prohibitions.

"For a child of Adventist parents, Sabbath can sometimes seem like a day of don'ts and can'ts—can't watch TV, can't ride your bike, can't play with certain toys or read certain books," he says. "For me, the focus of Sabbath should be on developing a deeper awareness of God's presence in the world and in my life. Sabbath is also an opportunity to reach out to others. But it's hard to know how much children can be expected to appreciate this.

"Children are often not very reflective or altruistic beings—mine aren't anyway—and basically, they don't get it. For me, a walk in the bush, a swim in the creek, or a bike ride along a back road are spiritual, reflective experiences—especially when done on Sabbath. But for my kids, the same activities are an opportunity to let off steam, to whoop and run, to splash and stunt. It's the most difficult dilemma about Sabbath for me. Do I ban them from these activities on Sabbath because they are clearly not entering into them with the correct mindset? Would I prefer that they sit at home feeling grumpy because they're not allowed to do anything? That's hardly a correct Sabbath state of mind either."

The struggle is one he's still working to resolve, Kent says. "The only solution I can see involves spending time with my kids in direct interaction."

Kent tries to take the time to point out the wonders of nature that they see on their afternoon walks. He also teaches his children through Bible quizzes, singing praise songs with them, even discussing spiritual topics "at a level they understand and for a time period their concentration can manage."

Part of passing on a Sabbath tradition to your children requires a bit of trust and patience. "I try to remember that they're just kids; they haven't made a personal decision for Jesus yet, let alone decided on how they view Sabbath. I would like them to learn, however, that Sabbath is a precious gift from God which can add much to your lifestyle and spiritual experience."[8]

praying with the poor

As we've said, praying is not necessarily reciting words but listening. It's noticing where God is at work and then joining in that work. It is appropriate to do something to help the poor on Sabbath or to serve others. Our care for the poor extends to them the shelter that God has given us.

Isaiah 58 talks about prayer and another spiritual discipline intimately linked with prayer—fasting. Through his prophet, God is reprimanding his people. "You cannot fast as you do today and expect your voice to be heard on high," he says in verse 4. Through this verse, we see the intimate link between fasting and prayer.

The point of fasting and repentance is not to demand things of God but to identify with the oppressed. "Is not this the kind of fasting I have chosen: to loose the chains of injustice and untie the cords of the yoke, to set the oppressed free and break every yoke? Is it not to share your food with the hungry and to provide the poor wanderer with shelter — when you see the naked, to clothe them?" (Isa. 58:6–7).

Marva Dawn writes, "The Sabbath is a day for sharing, for gifting others in many ways, for knowing that the Lord of the Sabbath provides abundantly for us so that we can, in turn, be generous."[9]

Who finds it easier to be generous? A person who has much? Or a person who (although he may actually have less) believes he has more than enough?

Isaiah 58 is all about that generosity. This same chapter tells us that Sabbath is a delight, but not one that is found by "going your own way" (v. 13). When we honor the Lord's Day by loving others, we will find joy. This is the call of Sabbath delight: to go God's way, which is a way of compassion.

One Sunday, my kids and I spent part of our Sabbath day "spending ourselves in behalf of the poor" (see Isa. 58:10). A few weeks prior, we had gone to church on a Wednesday evening to worship and to help fill and wrap gift boxes for underprivileged families and nursing-home patients. The kids got into the assembly-line nature of the project, and Melanie, twelve at the time, was excited to be allowed to be at the wrapping station, wrapping with brightly colored holiday paper the cardboard boxes we'd filled with hand lotion, snacks, and other necessities.

So on Sunday, when those same boxes were delivered to a

nursing home, we went to help distribute them to the residents. My kids brought a friend each, and we joined others from our church. We delivered each box to a resident, sang Christmas carols to them (oftentimes with them, as they joined in), and said a prayer for each one who accepted our offer to do so.

At dinner that night, we talked about the experience. Some of the people had been a bit scary—with a goiter on the neck or a pant leg that crept up on an artificial limb. The smells, despite the cleanliness of the facility, were, well, unusual and pungent. The rooms were kept at tropical heat levels, so that all the children were flushed and the younger ones a bit sleepy.

At dinner, we read a bit of Isaiah 58 and talked about how God calls us to make the Sabbath not just about ourselves and our rest but about God.

"I thought Sabbath was a day for me to relax," Melanie said.

"It's a day to take a break from our regular work so we can be refreshed, yes," I said. "But it's also a day to care about the things God cares about, to focus on him, and to show his love to others. So today you spent part of your Sabbath the way the Bible says you should—not just going your own way but going God's way. And God's way often takes us to people who are poor or lonely or sick."

Some families I spoke to choose to make serving the poor a part of their weekly Sabbath; others just do it occasionally. Serving a meal at a soup kitchen might be an excellent activity to try as part of your Sabbath practice.

the economics of the Sabbath

Why serve the poor on Sabbath? Because Sabbath is more than a day. It's a mindset that informs not only spiritual practice but economic realities. Exodus 23 is all about a Sabbath-style economic policy. It instructs God's people not only to keep a weekly Sabbath but also, every seventh year, to give the land a Sabbath rest. The reason for this is not just wise agricultural practice but to provide a tangible reminder of God's deep concern for the poor.

The Bible says, "For six years you are to sow your fields and harvest the crops, but during the seventh year let the land lie unplowed and unused. Then the poor among your people may get food from it, and the wild animals may eat what they leave. Do the same with your vineyard and your olive grove. Six days do your work, but on the seventh day do not work, so that your ox and your donkey may rest and the slave born in your household, and the foreigner among you as well, may be refreshed" (Exod. 23:10–12).

This should not be interpreted to mean we ought to care for the poor only every seventh year. Rather, as we remember the Sabbath and imitate God by keeping it, we should also imitate God by caring even for those who serve us by allowing them to rest and find refreshment.

Ched Myers writes, "The Sabbath thus captures the double theme of the creation story: abundance as divine gift, and self-limitation as the appropriate response."[10]

living a Sabbath life

If we live a life of Sabbath Simplicity, we don't rest all the time. In fact, we work six days out of seven. "Six days shall you labor and do all your work" is how the command to Sabbath rest begins.

What does that work look like in your world? I think our work in the world has meaning when it is informed by our Sabbath practice. Sabbath is a mindset and a philosophy, a way of life that brings life to us.

This is the heart of Sabbath—to remember that freedom is

a gift. To observe Shabbat means to live it out, to care for the poor. To follow Jesus means that we take on his values. What is important to him ought to be important to us.

Isaiah 58, which is a part of traditional Jewish Shabbat liturgy, ends with a description of what happens when we "call the Sabbath a delight." But the beginning of the chapter (and for Jews, to cite one verse is to allude to its larger context) talks about another practice—fasting. And God says, "I don't really care about your practices if your heart is full of anger and strife" (see Isa. 58:3–5). The purpose of fasting is to have extra to share: "to share your food with the hungry and to provide the poor wanderer with shelter" (Isa. 58:7).

Therein lies the fundamental difference between Shabbat and mere leisure. Sabbath is not a day just to chill out and relax, although that may be part of it. It's a day to cultivate gratitude, which should lead us to generosity. It is a spiritual practice, meant to transform our hearts. The heart of the Sabbath commandment is freedom, not just for those who practice it but also for all people. The call to Sabbath is a call to social justice, which is what makes it especially relevant today, as the church grapples with issues of racism, poverty, disease, and our response to these ills.

God's Sabbath mentality is steeped in a rich tradition. Beyond calling the children of Israel to rest every seventh day, God called them to a Sabbath mentality every seventh year and, beyond that, every forty-ninth year (seven times seven) to celebrate a jubilee. In this Year of Jubilee, debts were cancelled, those who had sold themselves into slavery to pay off debts were released, and land was returned to its original owner. In other words, the hierarchy of society was flattened.

Myers writes, "We Christians therefore trivialize (and even 'profane') the Sabbath if we regard it merely as a day to do as little as possible, or as an antiquated Jewish code of nit-picking prohibitions. Torah's Sabbath regulations represent God's strategy for teaching Israel about its dependence upon the land as a gift to share equitably, not as a possession to exploit.... Sabbath observation means to remember every week this economy's two principles: the goal of 'enough' for everyone, and the prohibition on accumulation."[11]

The reminder that we once were slaves (in Egypt, or to sin) is also a call to compassion for the oppressed and to generosity. We have much in common with those who are in need, and we are called to keep that connection alive by being generous. Sabbath-keeping affirms that we have enough, that on this day, we don't need to work and accumulate money and goods. And if I have enough, then I am able to give to others. This is a key part of Sabbath practice. We are to take "enough" manna and leave the rest for others.

Our culture, in contrast, seems to have accumulation as its primary goal. We're taught to desire a bigger house, a nicer car, more stuff.

We are consumers, and the more we have, the more we are in danger of being blind to the impact of our consumption. And yet, like Solomon, we sometimes feel that all this accumulation is "vanity" and does not really make us happy.

praying with your family

One of my mentors, Sibyl, is now an empty nester. But as her children were growing up, she did various things to make Sabbath special.

"I never always did the same thing," she says. "We kept it varied. But it was always a day focused on family."

First Samuel 7:12 tells about the nation of Israel fighting off the Philistine army. Samuel, their leader, acknowledged this miraculous victory by building an altar to commemorate the battle. "Then Samuel took a stone and set it up between Mizpah and Shen. He named it Ebenezer [which means "stone of help"], saying, 'Thus far the LORD has helped us.'"

So sometimes on Sundays, when Sibyl and her husband, Dick, gathered their children (and often, guests who were living at their house temporarily) around the table for dinner, they'd pull out a bowl with smooth stones in it. They'd read the story from 1 Samuel and then give each person a stone, noting that they were Ebenezer stones, meaning "God has helped us thus far." Then they'd ask each person to answer the question, "Where has God helped us this week?" As each child and adult told their story, they would place their stone in the bowl, thereby building a little altar of remembrance to remind each other that God does help and will always help.

We are hardwired to love stories. And this simple exercise is a way to let people tell their stories. It's a way of praying with children without droning on, without eyes closed. It invites participation, rather than demanding stillness from restless children. It asks us to engage, rather than just to be quiet.

When we answer the questions, Where has God helped us? Where have you noticed him? we are reminded of his work in our lives and how we joined in that work. We are gathering evidence, solid as stones, to confirm what we long to know: he is helping us; he is worthy of our praise.

"Make at least one meal with just your family part of Sabbath," Sibyl says. "Family-gathering reminds you that you belong to a clan. You are not isolated."

Sibyl says sometimes they would hold a family worship time on Sunday evening. Each person had to bring something—it could be an object, a Bible verse, a song, a story about how they'd seen God that week—anything that they could share with the family and that would help all of them worship together. "You have more buy-in when everyone contributes something," she says. Other times they would look at family videos together or cook a meal together. Choose activities based on the interest of your family.

pray without ceasing

Prayer is an integral part of our Sabbath practice, but it is not limited to Sabbath. The Bible tells us to pray without ceasing. How can we do that?

In his video *Breathe*, pastor Rob Bell points out that the ancient Jewish name for God, which our Bible translates as LORD (all caps), was actually four Hebrew vowels put together to represent the name of God (Yahweh). But because the name was so sacred, it was actually unpronounceable. Saying the four vowels one at a time, you get something like "Yahweh," or "Yah, hey, vod, hey." The name of God, he points out, is the sound of breathing.

Which makes sense, because in both Hebrew and Greek, the words for breath and spirit are the same word. In Hebrew, *ruah*. In Greek, *pneuma*.

Every day, we breathe without ceasing, whether we think about it or not. Breathing is both an involuntary action and one we can temporarily override, which is sort of amazing. We can breathe faster or slower. We can hold our breath. We can take a deep breath. But often we just breathe and don't even notice. We breathe shallowly, not breathing to our full potential and, thus, not receiving the energy and strength that breathing could provide, if only we'd learn how to do it.

Just as we are often not conscious of our breathing, we are often unaware of God. This does not negate God's existence, anymore than our lack of attention means we have stopped breathing. Rather, both instances tell us something about our level of perception. Becoming aware of God is like becoming aware of our breathing. We simply need to be quiet and pay attention.

Jesus said that we ought not to worry, and I believe that much of our hurried lifestyle comes from fear and worry — worry that we won't have enough, worry about impressing others, worry about getting things done. But Jesus says don't worry. If we don't worry, what should we do? "But seek first his kingdom and his righteousness, and all these things will be given to you as well" (Matt. 6:33). Or as Eugene Peterson renders this verse, "Steep your life in God-reality, God-initiative, God-provisions. Don't worry about missing out. You'll find all your everyday human concerns will be met" (MSG).

What would happen if every time you found yourself hyperventilating, you took a moment just to breathe a little more slowly? Just to say the name of God and to take a deep breath? To remind yourself that God is as close as the air you breathe and to "steep your life in God-reality"? What if, whenever you found yourself distracted or stressed, you learned simply to breathe in the presence of God, which is all around you, and to listen to the voice of love? Wouldn't that listening be praying? Taking a moment simply to rest, a small Sabbath moment, a restful interlude in which you gave your attention to God — if you did this several times a day, made it a practice, I'm guessing your life might begin to look different. That kind of prayer could, if you let it, transform your life.

What if you saw every breath as a gift from God? What if "pray without ceasing" is not about talking at God but about listening to God or simply noticing that everything that has breath is praising the LORD, because everything that breathes is saying his name: "Yah, hey, vod, hey"?

Prayer is a way that we live in Sabbath Simplicity not just one day a week but every day.

the sweetest Sabbaths

As I mentioned earlier, keeping Sabbath the last few Sundays before this book was due challenged my ability to trust. To be honest, it was not easy. Knowing I had an unfinished manuscript on my hard drive and a book deadline a few weeks away made it hard to take a day away from the computer.

But I chose to practice what I preach. I decided to trust God and give him those days. And I have to tell you, these few weeks have been the sweetest Sabbaths of all. Gentle dinners shared with my family as the last light fades in an autumn sky. Quiet Sundays on the couch in front of the fire, talking or playing board games with my children. The trip to the museum with my son. Talks and cuddling with my husband. Ordinary moments in which I said loudly with my quiet actions, "I trust you, God." They were the sweetest Sabbaths I had experienced in a long time because I chose to trust, knowing it cost me something. And on Mondays, my productivity soared—God gave me ideas, words. My writing was ignited.

When you give God a little time, he gives you back far more than you could ever imagine. Inspiration, strength for your tasks, help from unexpected people and places. He brought me just the right people, resources, and experiences to finish the book.

It's now after sunset on the last Sabbath before I finish this book. I'm trusting I'll finish it this week. I've spent the last twenty-four hours focused on relationships with others and with God, not on my work. At sunset last night, I watched the moon rise and enjoyed a simple meal with my family. I slept well. This morning I woke before the alarm and spent an hour in quiet, then went to church with my family. After church, I baked pumpkin bread for my neighbor Joel and his daughters. I'd received an email earlier in the week from another neighbor, telling me a group of our neighbors planned to put up Christmas decorations at Joel's home. We did the same thing last year, making their home the brightest on the street, perhaps in the whole subdivision. Because last year, Joel's wife, Amy, was dying of cancer. Dozens of neighbors gathered in her yard, bringing hot chocolate and decorations, hoping to brighten the spirits of a family going through an awful time.

This year, we decorated without Amy — at least, without her physical presence, since she died not long after last Christmas. But although she wasn't present physically, we felt her spirit close to all of us. A crowd of neighbors and friends gathered again, decorating the trees and house. Someone set up a sound system with Christmas carols; kids helped themselves to cookies that people brought and set out on a table in the driveway. We were just putting up Christmas decorations, chatting with neighbors. There was a sort of defiant joy in the air. Joel and the girls were helping with all of the work. Several of the guys were on the roof stringing lights. People laughed, visited, caught up with folks they'd been too busy to talk to for months. My fingers were numb after an hour, but I didn't care. God was there as we all loved on each other, as we let the shekhinah of God shine on our neighbors.

I would not have missed this afternoon, hanging ornaments in the thirty-degree weather, for anything. We got to stop. Together. We all stopped from our many other activities, at least for a while. Many of my neighbors would look at me quizzically if I asked them about Sabbath. Some of them don't even go to church regularly. But because they loved Amy, and they love her family, they chose to stop this Sunday. To set aside other tasks, for a little while, so they could love in action and in truth. In so doing, we created a little tabernacle where God could dwell, where love could dwell.

It was a moment of sacramental ordinary, if ever one existed. And although I went thinking I was one who was giving, I also received in abundance. I was so thankful for the gift of Sabbath.

Whatever you do, don't miss the gift.

acknowledgments

One of the joys of being a writer is that you connect, through words, with people you'd never have met otherwise. You put your soul on a page and pray—and mostly, you never find out what happens. Sales numbers just can't provide that much detail.

But sometimes, readers will connect with your words, will recognize a bit of themselves in what you say, or possibly even be changed in some small way. If the connection is deep and strong enough, they'll make some effort to complete the circuit by sending some words back, via a letter or email.

It is those readers, the ones who turned my monologue into a conversation, that I wish to thank. Many shared their stories for this book, to keep the conversation going. Others just said thanks, which is plenty.

I also am deeply grateful to the team at Zondervan, who have embraced this project and worked to make it the best it could be. Thanks especially to editors Angela Scheff and Brian Phipps, who challenged me to clarify my thinking and carefully honed my writing.

Thanks also to my wonderful agent, Chip MacGregor, who took me on as a client when my career had seemingly lost momentum. He saw the potential in this project and provided some much-needed encouragement and no-nonsense career guidance that got me back on track. He's always believed in me, and that is no small gift.

Thanks also to Bob Gordon, who offered great advice and encouragement after reading an early draft.

Finally, I want to thank my husband, Scot, and my wonderful kids, Melanie and Aaron. When a wife and mother is also a writer, her family makes some sacrifices, and mine have made many. They've encouraged me, each in their own way. They've not complained too much when deadlines took priority over making dinner or cleaning. They've embraced (mostly out of necessity) a team approach to chores and running the house. They've reminded me to laugh and inspired me to pray. My ministry would not be possible without their love and support, and I'm grateful.

reading
group guide

"In spiritual rest, we recover our lives. We discover the gift of community with people and with our Creator, and the depth, texture, and richness that gift adds to our lives. We get a chance to stop, turn, and really notice the faces of the people running through life beside us and to feel grateful for them. This is no small gift" (from chapter 2).

This guide was created to enhance your reading of *Rest: Living in Sabbath Simplicity*. You can use it on your own if you like. But because Sabbath is, at its heart, a communal discipline, I recommend that you find even just one or two other people to connect with as you reflect on your reading.

You are embarking on a journey toward Sabbath Simplicity. The focus is not on the destination but on the journey itself. I recommend that each group member keep a journal, to record observations, questions that come up, quotes from the book, quotes from other sources. Use it to do some of the exercises in this study guide.

Since Sabbath itself is a weekly practice, you may want to meet weekly while reading the book. Since the book's chapters are rather lengthy, I suggest that you spend two weeks on each chapter. At that pace, reading about half a chapter for each meeting, the book will take you approximately three months to read.

When you gather, agree on a few simple rules: keep confidential what's shared in meetings. Encourage one another. Refrain from giving heavy-handed advice, from attempting to fix each other. Leave the fixing to God, but ask each other honest questions. Don't force everyone to answer every question; allow each person to share at the level they feel comfortable with. Make the group a safe place.

You may want to start your meetings with this simple question: Where did you notice God since we last met? For example, we may notice God in an answer to prayer, in an encounter with a stranger, in a situation at work, in our actual Sabbath practice. Try to answer as specifically as you can. Knowing that you will be asked that question will help you to remember during the week to pay attention, to notice, to *see*, as Elizabeth Barrett Browning writes,

> *Earth's crammed with heaven*
> *And every common bush afire with God;*
> *But only he who sees, takes off his shoes—*
> *The rest sit round it and pluck blackberries.*

If you get stuck or have questions, visit www.keriwyattkent.com and leave a note. I'll try to answer as many questions as I can on my blog.

chapter 1: shaking things up

1. What has been your experience with the practice of Sabbath? What were Sundays like in your family as a kid? What are they like for you now? What is one thing you'd like to change about the way you spend your Sabbath?

2. Read the first two pages of the chapter, which explore what was meant by a rabbi's "yoke" in Jesus' day. What was Jesus' yoke? Consider the following words from Jesus: "Come to me, all you who are weary and burdened, and I will give you rest. Take my yoke upon you and learn from me, for I am gentle and humble in heart, and you will find rest for your souls. For my yoke is easy and my burden is light" (Matt. 11:28–30). What did Jesus mean when he said "my yoke is easy"?

3. Read the first Sabbath story from Mark's gospel (Mark 1:21–34). As you read, imagine yourself as one of Jesus' disciples. Observe what happens in the synagogue and then what happens when you return to Peter's home. What do you notice about Jesus? If you could enjoy a Sabbath afternoon with Jesus, what would you like to talk to him about?

4. Read the second and third Sabbath stories from Mark's gospel (Mark 2:23–28; 3:1–6). Why do you think the Pharisees disliked Jesus so much?

5. What holds you in bondage? Are you a slave to your to-do list? Are you imprisoned by your schedule? Have your activities and busyness become your taskmaster? What is one thing you could do to change that?

chapter 2: resting

We are restless people, driven not only from within but also from without. Our culture thrives on hurry and venerates the busy. But our bodies and souls are injured by our hurried lifestyles. We long for rest but will find it only in the presence of God.

1. In what ways are you restless?

2. Describe the pace of your life. Do you have times when you unplug and relax? Do you normally get enough sleep each night? Do you have trouble sleeping?

3. How have you stretched yourself lately? Did you give yourself time to recover after you exerted yourself? Do you fully engage and fully disengage in activities during your day?

4. Read this statement: "When I relax, I feel guilty." On a scale of one to five, how true is this of you?

5. Complete this sentence, if it resonates with you: "Sabbath-keeping is impossible for me because ..." If you are willing, allow group members to give you honest feedback about what they see in your life.

chapter 3: reconnecting

In this chapter, we talk about the roots of our faith and how understanding and embracing that heritage can deepen our faith. Reconnecting with others is a part of Sabbath that will soothe our disconnectedness and isolation.

1. What is your response to the story of Herb and Rae Lowe? What appeals to you about their Sabbath practice? What do you not like about it?

2. Describe a time when you felt isolated from others. If that is your situation, what contributes to that feeling? What is one thing you could do on Sabbath to connect with others?

3. What Sabbath-keeping tradition did you grow up in? How does your church community celebrate the Sabbath? What Sabbath practices would help you show love to God and those around you?

4. How does looking at Jewish and Christian history shape your understanding and practice of Sabbath?

5. What day do you plan to observe Sabbath?

6. How does your church community either support or hinder your attempts at Sabbath-keeping?

chapter 4: revising

Living in Sabbath Simplicity requires us to make some changes. While it is not always easy to revise, it is what we need when we feel stuck and want to escape.

1. Describe a place in your life where you feel "stuck."

2. What does your Sabbath look like right now? What next steps in your Sabbath Simplicity journey do you sense God is calling you to? What revisions would you need to make to take that step?

3. What activities would you like to refrain from (be set free from) on Sabbath?

4. What rituals are currently a part of your weekly routine? (These don't necessarily have to be religious—a nightly soak in the tub is a ritual, as is watching a favorite television show.) What rituals do you want to include in your life? What rituals could you incorporate into your Sabbath?

5. What could you do during the week to prepare to rest on the Sabbath?

chapter 5: pausing

Before we can learn to take a day off, we may have to begin with learning to take a minute off. We live in a 24/7 world and have forgotten how to pause. But it is in the pauses that we find the meaning and the beauty in life.

1. Describe a typical day. Do you have time to pause in the midst of it?

2. Write out your weekly schedule. How do you spend the hours of your day? How much time do work, chores, and family time take up? How many hours are you in the car? You may want to put it in chart form, using colors for various activities. Put a normal week (including kids' activities, if applicable) onto one page. Notice some trends. How many hours do you spend doing chores? How many hours are you in the car? What would you like to cut out? Are there places you could substitute relational time for activities that tend to separate you from others? (For example, could you cut out one of your child's many activities and substitute a regular family activity?)

3. Are the people you live with or work with hectic or frazzled? How much of your pace of life is driven by the demands of others? What boundaries would you like to set to avoid getting drawn into their panic?

4. Over the next few days, notice how often you multitask. Do you feel more focused and efficient when you do so? Does anything get your full attention?

5. Set aside an hour or more during which you will do one thing at a time. Afterward, write down a few sentences about how you felt during that time.

6. What is your response to Tahna's story? Can you relate to her situation? How would it affect your relationships if you began to clearly communicate your expectations and what others can expect from you?

chapter 6: playing

Sabbath and play are intertwined. If we stop working on Sabbath, it gives us time to play. But can that play draw us toward God? Can workaholics and people addicted to accomplishment find a way to play that doesn't turn into intense competition?

1. What do you think Jesus meant when he said we should be like children?

2. Discuss these questions from the chapter: What rejuvenates you? If you had some time to do something you enjoy, what would that be?

3. Gather your family around the table for a meal and ask, "If we had a family day, what are some things you'd like to do?" Are you a family that enjoys exploring museums or going to the beach or a local pool? Do you like playing board games or going out on excursions? Do you like reading or listening to stories? Do you prefer being inside or outside, active or relaxed? Write down suggestions for family time on slips of paper. Select one each week and do it on the Sabbath.

4. How do you understand the difference between *chronos* and *kairos* time? Tell about a time when you were in kairos time.

5. Ginger said she'd rather clean house than just play with the kids. Is this you? Or are you more inclined toward play? (Or do you define play in another way, such as doing things you like?) How easy is it for you to just goof off?

chapter 7: praying

Prayer is more than just talking to God; it's a means to fueling our relationship with God. It includes speaking, listening, and acting on what God tells us. It is the antidote for our self-importance and self-absorption.

1. Do you feel Twenge's assessment of her own generation is accurate? Are you a part of Generation Me? Are your children?

2. Prior to reading this chapter, how would you have defined prayer? How has this chapter changed your understanding?

3. If God is spirit, why did God command his people to build a tabernacle? Do you think God still wants to dwell among us? Do you have sufficient space in your life for God?

4. Explain the link between Sabbath and tabernacle. What truth about God can you draw from what you've learned? Brainstorm some ways you could serve the poor, lonely, or sick on the Sabbath.

5. What is your response to the story of Kent Kingston and his family? What can you learn from them?

notes

chapter 1: shaking things up

1. Rob Bell, *Velvet Elvis* (Grand Rapids: Zondervan, 2005), 47.
2. Ibid., 48–49.
3. Norman Wirzba, *Living the Sabbath* (Grand Rapids: Brazos, 2006), 43.

chapter 2: resting

1. Jim Loehr and Tony Schwartz, *The Power of Full Engagement* (New York: Free Press, 2003), 37.
2. Ibid., 38.
3. Ibid., 32.
4. These stats are from www.sleepfoundation.org. Past years' reports have focused on other population groups.
5. This info is from www.apollohealth.com, although you could find similar information in a science textbook or other websites.
6. 2002 *Sleep in America* poll, www.sleepfoundation.org.
7. The study results were on www.medco.com in a news release dated April 30, 2007. Several commentaries on other sites pointed out that drug companies are profiting from the increasing trend toward popping sleeping pills.
8. Randy Frazee, *Making Room for Life* (Grand Rapids: Zondervan, 2003), 18.
9. Ibid., 63.
10. Loehr and Schwartz, *The Power of Full Engagement*, 13.

11. Henri Nouwen, "Moving from Solitude to Community," *Leadership*, Spring 1995, http://www.ctlibrary.com/14810.

12. Rainer Maria Rilke, *Letters to a Young Poet* (New York: Random House, 1984; Modern Library Edition, 2001), 78.

chapter 3: reconnecting

1. Mark Buchanan, *The Rest of God* (Nashville: W Publishing Group, 2006), 90.

2. Craig Harline, *Sunday: A History of the First Day from Babylonia to the Super Bowl* (New York: Doubleday, 2007), 97. Harline's book provides a fascinating history of how Sabbath traditions have evolved.

3. Murray Rothbard, *Conceived in Liberty*, vol. 1 (1975; Auburn, AL: Mises Institute, 1999), 174–81.

4. Tilden Edwards, *Sabbath Time* (Nashville: Upper Room, 1992), 45.

5. Dorothy Bass, *Receiving the Day* (San Francisco: Jossey-Bass, 2000), 48.

6. Ibid.

7. Keri Wyatt Kent, *Breathe: Creating Space for God in a Hectic Life* (Grand Rapids: Revell, 2005), 176.

8. Tracey R. Rich is a law librarian and practicing Jew who has developed a helpful "Judaism 101" website: www.jewfaq.org/shabbat.htm.

9. Buchanan, *The Rest of God*, 87.

10. From www.jewfaq.org/shabbat.htm.

11. Rob Bell, *Velvet Elvis* (Grand Rapids: Zondervan, 2005), 52, 54.

12. From www.jewfaq.org/shabbat.htm. This site is helpful for learning more about the life of both ancient and modern Jews.

13. Buchanan, *The Rest of God*, 93.

14. Harline, *Sunday*, 3.

15. Ibid., 6.

16. Ibid.

17. Most commentaries I checked agree that Hebrews was penned in the first century, likely before 70 AD.

18. See Robert Mulholland's book *Invitation to a Journey* (Downers Grove, IL: InterVarsity, 1993), 12.

19. I found this letter quoted on several websites, in various versions or translations. See chapter 9 in www.pseudepigrapha.com/LostBooks/ignatius2magnesians.htm, or earlychristianwritings.com.

20. Harline, *Sunday*, 91.

21. Ibid., 94.

22. Ibid., 91.

23. Karen Mains, *Making Sunday Special* (Waco, TX: Word, 1987), 21.

chapter 4: revising

1. Thomas Merton, *Conjectures of a Guilty Bystander* (New York: Doubleday, 1996), 73.

chapter 5: pausing

1. Check www.salary.com, or http://mom.salary.com.

2. Check out www.kindermusik.com if you'd like more information on this program.

3. Keri Wyatt Kent, *Breathe: Creating Space for God in a Hectic Life* (Grand Rapids: Revell, 2005), 213.

4. Groppel is the cofounder of the Human Performance Institute with Jim Loehr, whose work studying tennis players I cited in an earlier chapter.

5. Wayne Muller, *How, Then, Shall We Live?* (New York: Bantam, 1996), 227.

6. Marva Dawn, *Keeping the Sabbath Wholly* (Grand Rapids: Eerdmans, 1989), 20.

7. Ibid., 24.

8. "IKEA Peeks into Our Homes to See What We're Up To," *Chicago Tribune*, September 16, 2007, 5A (Q section).

9. Norman Shawchuck and Reuben Job, *A Guide to Prayer for All Who Seek God* (Nashville: Upper Room, 2003), 15.

10. Ibid.

11. Devin Brown, "Marvelous and Yet Not Strange: Tolkien's Sacramental Ordinary," in *Towards or Back to Human Values? Spiritual and Moral Dimensions of Contemporary Fantasy*, eds. Justina Deszcz-Tryhubczak and Marek Oziewicz (Newcastle, UK: Cambridge Scholars Press, 2006), 1, 3.

12. Mark Buchanan, *The Holy Wild* (Sisters, OR: Multnomah, 2003), 219.

chapter 6: playing

1. Brennan Manning, *The Importance of Being Foolish* (San Francisco: HarperSanFrancisco, 2005), 29–30.

2. Tilden Edwards, *Sabbath Time* (Nashville: Upper Room, 1992), 16.

3. Abraham J. Heschel, *The Sabbath: Its Meaning for Modern Man* (Boston: Shambhala, 1951), xvii.

4. Joseph Tkach and Neil Earle, "What Time Is It?" ChristianOdyssey.org, 2005, www.christianodyssey.org/gospel/time.htm.

5. Madeleine L'Engle, *Walking on Water* (New York: Bantam, 1980), 98.

6. Heschel, *The Sabbath*, 21.

7. I highly recommend Ginger Garrett's two novels, *Chosen: The Lost Diaries of Queen Esther* and *Dark Hour.*

8. Wayne Muller, *Sabbath: Restoring the Sacred Rhythm of Rest* (New York: Bantam, 1999), 137.

chapter 7: praying

1. Jean M. Twenge, *Generation Me* (New York: Free Press, 2006), 4.

2. For more detail on how to listen to God, I humbly recommend my previous book, *Listen: Finding God in the Story of Your Life* (San Francisco: Jossey-Bass, 2006).

3. Wayne Muller, *Sabbath: Restoring the Sacred Rhythm of Rest* (New York: Bantam, 1999), 26.

4. From Manfred Schreyer's website, www.spiritrestoration.org. Used with permission.

5. Ibid.

6. For a complete list, see Tracey Rich's helpful Judaism 101 website. This page has the entire list of thirty-nine, plus lots of other great information: www.jewfaq.org/shabbat.htm.

7. From www.aish.com/shabbatthemes/explorations/Tabernacle_of_Time.asp.

8. Kent shared his story with me via email. I respect his practice and admire much of it, even though it differs from mine — I rest on a different day, and I think letting children "blow off steam and whoop and run" is completely acceptable Sabbath practice. However, I think even when we have different opinions about some things, we can still learn from each other. His and other stories in this book are not meant to provide formulas but are meant to provide an opportunity to learn from one another.

9. Marva Dawn, *Keeping the Sabbath Wholly* (Grand Rapids: Eerdmans, 1989), 146.

10. Ched Myers, *The Biblical Vision of Sabbath Economics*, Tell the Word series (Washington, D.C.: Church of the Saviour, 2001), 11.

11. Ibid., 13.

Read this excerpt from
Keri Wyatt Kent's next book:

Simple Compassion

Devotions to Make a Difference in Your Neighborhood and Your World

"He has shown all you people what is good. And what does the Lord require of you? To act justly, to love mercy, and to walk humbly with your God" (Micah 6:8). When I first heard this verse, I was in my early twenties, coming back into the church after a few years of, well, not being in the church. In all my childhood years of memorizing and studying the Bible, I don't remember hearing it. But I wasn't sure how to live that verse. It sounded so simple. But I was still trying to make some space in my life for God. I found it immensely challenging just to do the "walk humbly" part, since for several years my life had been almost entirely focused on myself. "Stumble proudly" was accurate of me.

I think God wants us to live a life that matters not just to ourselves but to the world. He wants for us to put our faith into action. And not just by what I grew up calling "witnessing" —talking about Jesus. What if the witnessing you did with your actions was just as important as the witnessing you did with your mouth? After all, Jesus declared loving God and loving your neighbor his "top two" commandments.

I realized that if I was truly being spiritually transformed, my actions and attitudes would be changed as well. Jesus was compassionate, not necessarily in a "nice" way but in a "confront the social order, care about justice for the poor and the marginalized" sort of way. If the goal of Christian spiritual formation is to become more Christlike, then I should be more compassionate, more concerned for fighting against injustice.

It almost seemed as if walking humbly with God would result in transformation of my attitudes and my actions, that if I really were walking humbly with him, I would begin to love mercy and to act justly. These three strands intertwine into a single cord.

To open this book, and read just one short chapter a week, is to offer God a year to mess with you, to equip and strengthen you to live the adventure of following him, to let go of being too busy and bored, all at the same time, and really start living your faith. This book is a guide toward becoming a more compassionate person, a person who doesn't just talk about faith, or social justice, but is trying to live it out. Compassion flows from those who are so full of God's love that it simply sloshes onto everyone around them. When we act justly and love mercy, it strengthens our walk with God. And when we walk with God, it leads us to love mercy (because we have been shown mercy) and to act justly (because we are becoming more like Jesus).

Over the next year, you'll get some practical guidance on really loving your neighbors, both those next door and those around the world. We'll look at what the Bible says about how we are to respond to poverty and suffering, and offer small steps you can take to grow in compassion for the poor and the marginalized. We'll listen to the stories of a variety of believers who have taken steps to grow in compassion and courage.

Using this book is easy. Each week, read a chapter. They're short stories, really, about my life and about the lives of people

I've met through my work as a journalist and a writer. Some are stories about women from history—including the Bible. And each story has Scripture woven in. During the week, reflect on what you've read. Maybe write the verses or quotes from the chapter in a journal or on note cards that you can carry around with you. Pray about what you've read. Then every chapter ends with two action steps. The first is an individual compassion step —a question to get you thinking or something you can do to make a difference, to shine a light in the darkness of your neighborhood, your city, your world. The second is a community step. The Christian life is meant to be lived in community, and I hope that you are a part of a group of people who know, pray for, and care for each other. The community step will provide ways for groups to interact with this book, to discuss it, and to live out what they are learning.

This book is an invitation to make your life more interesting. Full disclosure also would require me to say that "interesting" might also include "messy" or "complex." But it also might mean "focused" and "meaningful." I want to help us to find a life that overflows with joy, a life that shines the light of Christ everywhere.

So if you are interested in a life of greater, I don't know … texture or adventure, welcome. I'm inviting you to join me on a journey, a journey toward a deeper life, a deeper joy. A journey in which you will begin to see how you can make a difference—and what a thrill it is to show God's love to others. A journey in which you discover that you can live a life that matters. Let's walk humbly with God together.

If you like, visit me online (www.keriwyattkent.com) as you're reading, and let me know how those action steps are going. My hope is that as you read, you will be infused with confidence and strength to change the world, one life at a time. Starting with your own. ❖

Keri Wyatt Kent writes and speaks about the connection between faith and real life. Visit www.keriwyattkent.com, where you can learn more about her books and retreats, read her blog and newsletter, and find lots of helpful and encouraging information, including a free study guide for this book.

Keri is also the author of *Breathe: Creating Space for God in a Hectic Life* (Revell, 2005) and several other books. She and her husband, Scot, have been married seventeen years and live with their son and daughter in Illinois.